Teaching Kids
to Spell:

A Developmental
Approach to Spelling

Becky Spence

http://www.ThisReadingMama.com

Teaching Kids to Spell: A Developmental Approach to Spelling

Editing and design services by Melinda Martin of
http://www.TheHelpyHelper.com.

This book is dedicated to:

First, to my Heavenly Father. With You, I am more than a conqueror. Without You, I am nothing. Thank You for giving me the passion of teaching. It is a true blessing from You.

To my husband, Jason. Thank you for the hours you've watched the kids so I could "finish my book", which never seemed "done." I love you and am thankful for you.

To my four little blessings. I am blessed to have you call me "mommy",
even if it's five hundred times a day!

To Dr. Francine Johnston, who gave me my first taste of teaching spelling through the word study approach.

Table of Contents

Introduction

Spelling is one of those subjects that seems mysterious at times. The questions that surround the teaching of spelling are many and can also seem daunting. We know how we were taught spelling. For many of us, this may have included rote drills and spelling tests. We know we do not want to pass on the "drill and kill" legacy when it comes to teaching spelling, but what alternatives do we have? Can spelling really be hands-on and fun? What resources are available for teaching spelling? What should I expect from my child's spellings?

There are some very popular myths that surround spelling as well. You may have heard or even thought some these, such as:

■ Spelling is not as important as it used to be now that kids have spell check.

■ My child is a proficient reader, but his spelling lags behind his reading. Something is wrong with him.

■ English is so full of exceptions that kids can't make sense of it all.

■ Allowing kids to misspell words is never okay. They will not learn the correct spellings if we allow them to do this.

■ My child aces all his spelling tests, so he is a good speller.

■ Learning sight words is a better approach than learning phonics (or vice versa).

In this book, I hope to debunk some of the spelling myths as well as help you, the parent, understand your child's spellings. We will explore spelling development and hands-on ways that spelling can (and should) be taught. Hang on as we explore how to teach kids to spell!

Note: Some of the links in this book have been shortened. Even though they may look a little strange, they are valid.

Chapter 1: Why Kids Misspell Words

When speaking with parents about spelling over the years, I have heard many parents say, "My child is just a lazy speller." While kids do often try to take the short cut (if we are honest, many adults do, too), I would like to offer several reasons that kids misspell words. And a big hint: laziness is not one of my reasons.

Spelling is much more demanding than talking.

When a child in the younger primary grades draws a picture, we sit beside her and say, "Tell me about your picture." We sometimes listen for a full minute (if not more) as she explains her picture. We respond, "Awesome! Let's write a sentence about your picture now." The child looks at us in panic. How is she supposed to fit all of that into one sentence? (Yes, I'm being a little far-fetched with that example, but it is a reality.) As those young readers become older readers, we may ask a comprehension question, such as, "If you were that character, how would you have responded?" The reader orally shares a detailed plan. But ask that same reader to write her response and you may only get a sentence or two (if you are lucky). Writing and spelling are much more demanding. They take a lot more energy from the reader and can be a hindrance for some kids, especially reluctant writers.

3

Spelling is more demanding than reading.

While reading is a recognition task, spelling is a production task. This means spellers have to produce a product (a spelling), while readers only need to recognize what is already there. Because production tasks are more difficult, spelling development usually follows behind the development of word recognition (McKenna and Stahl, 2003). When we spell, we must produce the correct spellings, not merely recognize words. Spelling, even in adults, usually lags behind reading skills. For example, if you are reading and come across the word *miscellaneous*, you can read/recognize it without a problem. But spelling *miscellaneous* correctly leaves us at the mercy of spell check. The same is true of developing readers.

A beginning reader relies heavily on context clues (what would make sense in the sentence or picture clues) to figure out many words. Using those strategies, she is able to read those books with success because of all the support provided on the pages of that book. At this stage of literacy, spelling words will naturally be harder. Why? Because "more information is needed to produce a correct spelling than a correct reading. Failure to remember one or two letters dooms a perfect spelling, but not necessarily an accurate reading" (Ehri, 1997). What does spelling look like for a child in this stage? We will explore that topic in the next chapter.

As readers progress into the primary grades, the pictures begin to provide less support in figuring out the words. They must shift more to focus on the letters of the words to read. But readers, even at this stage, may not be paying attention to every single letter in a word to read it. They may only be using partial cues to read words. For example, they may use only the first and last letter to help them read a word, so *block* may be read as *back*. But still, readers typically read with high success, even if they do not pay attention to every single letter. And again, the act of spelling words conventionally requires more spelling strategies that the child does not yet possess.

As readers progress further, they begin to read by patterns or by analogy (meaning the child can come to an unknown word: *blight*, but can read it because he says, "Hmmm..., this unknown word has a word I know in it: *light*.") This is the stage in which reading really begins to take off. But when that same child sits down to write and spell, the spellings may be off a bit. Even though the child can read the word, she cannot spell it correctly. We scratch our heads and wonder what is going on. And once again, the blame lies in the fact that spelling requires more than the child has to offer. The same spelling patterns that the child can read become a bit ambiguous when the child wants to spell them. Take, just for example, the long *u* pattern. Long *u* can be spelled many ways: *ew, oo, ui, ue,* and *u_e* (not to mention the occasional *ou* like in *soup*). A reader may be able to successfully read every pattern, but when she needs to spell *juice* in her sentence, she has a lot of choices for spelling that long *u* spelling.

It is interesting to look at just what goes on in the head of a young writer. A young speller has to not only think of what he wants to write, but also how to:

- listen for letter sounds in each word (phonemes),

- pick the right letter/letter combination that matches each sound (phonics),

- remember what the letter(s) looks like (visualize),

- form each letter correctly (handwriting),

- remember the *exact order* in which the letters come to spell words conventionally (spelling), and

- remember what message he was trying to portray in the first place; so he can start the whole process all over again to spell the next word in his sentence.

Whew! I'm exhausted. How about you? No wonder it may take a young writer ten minutes just to write three words!

Correct spelling requires kids to have a certain level of letter-sound knowledge.

In order to spell, young spellers have to be able to hear the sounds within the word (phonemic awareness). Younger children will many times write down only the sounds they can "feel" in their mouth when they say the word. Typically, this is just the beginning or ending consonant. Vowels do not usually come until later. (If you're a skeptic, say *cat* out loud right now. Can you feel your mouth make the /k/ and /t/ sounds? How about the short *a* in the middle? It is not as prominent.) It is more likely that a child will misspell a word if he is not solid in (1) certain letter sounds or letter sound combinations (phonics) or (2) hearing/feeling the sounds within words (phonemic awareness).

Spelling is memorized instead of learned in a purposeful way.

"The goal of spelling instruction is to create fluent writers, not perfect scores on the spelling text" (Newlands, 2011). Many teachers and moms can attest to the fact that those same kids who aced that spelling test last Friday turn right around and misspell the same words on Monday! Spelling cannot be taught solely as a "memorize and regurgitate" subject. By teaching spelling in this way, we are unknowingly teaching random rules and spelling patterns without the logic that goes behind it. (Yes, you heard right. English spellings are mostly logical.)

"Spelling lists don't provide students with an understanding of *why* words are spelled certain ways, which would help students figure out how to spell the new words they encounter. And worse yet, lists can easily confuse the young spelling student, making the subject of spelling seem difficult and unlearnable" (http://bit.ly/1kbJmXF).

How are kids supposed to make sense of the English language other than to just memorize only to forget later? We will explore some strategies in Chapter 4.

Spelling "rules" are too heavily emphasized.

"When two vowels go walking, the first one does the talking." Ever heard that commonly used rule before? While "there are many reliable rules and generalizations in English spelling that will help students make the correct choices in their own writing," an over-emphasis of those rules can serve to confuse our kids (http://bit.ly/1ndN8Va).

There are three main reasons rule-based phonics instruction is not the best way to teach spelling. The **first**, and the most common reason, is that there are so many exceptions. The two-vowel example above does not take into account the multiple double vowel pairs in our language that do not follow this rule (such as *ou, oi, oy, ow,* short *ea, oo, aw,* and *au*). Teaching kids rules that are too easily broken focus more upon inconsistencies within the English language rather than consistencies. **Secondly**, if we teach spelling as simply a list of rules, we will find that there are too many rules for kids to remember. These rules can actually get in the way of decoding as kids are almost enslaved to the rules. **Lastly**, "teacher-taught rules seldom stick" (Invernizzi, Abouzeid & Bloodgood, 1997). Spellers need time to work with and manipulate words in spelling instruction that share a common pattern so they can be guided to develop a generalization or "rule" about the words with the adult's help. In Chapter 6, you will find ideas and suggestions for doing just this.

There is a Bigger Issue Going On

Because spelling requires more out of a child than reading, children who have a hard time learning letter sounds (phonics) or hearing sounds in words (phonemic awareness) will probably also struggle to spell. Children who have been diagnosed with dyslexia or other reading disorders will have a harder time with spelling. My encouragement to you is to make spelling as explicit, hands-on and multi-sensory as possible for these children. One particular company, *Reading with TLC* (http://www.readingwithtlc.com), specializes in helping children develop that ear for phonics and phonemic awareness with a multi-sensory curriculum called *Lively Letters*.

The Good News about Misspellings

In the 1970s, a few researchers (Charles Read, Carol Chomsky, and Edmund Henderson) took a long look at kids' misspellings. What they found was extraordinary. It actually changed the way researchers and spelling teachers look at spelling forever. Read, in particular, discovered that "preschoolers' [spelling] attempts were not just random displays of ignorance and confusion. To the contrary, his linguistic analysis showed that children's [misspellings] provided a window into their developing word knowledge" (Bear, et. al 2012).

The misspellings of our own child are not merely signs of his laziness. They are identification markers, giving us specific information towards his awareness of how letter sounds and phonics patterns work. "We can gain insight into a child's ability to read words by looking at how he/she spells words" (Morris, 2005). When we are able to look at our child's misspellings and analyze the information they provide, we are given a huge clue as to where our teaching of spelling should begin. We will explore this topic more in Chapter 2.

Chapter 2: Spelling Development

We can take a look at how kids naturally progress in their understanding of how words work by looking at their spellings/misspellings. This developmental progression of spelling is true of most spellers. Being able to identify your child's level of development is a wonderful way to ensure that your teaching of spelling is on target for your learner. "By determining what [your child] uses but confuses…you will learn which [spelling] features and patterns to explore, because this is where instruction will most benefit [your child]" (Bear, et. al 2012).

As we dive into spelling development, please note two things.

(1) While age ranges are included for each stage, your child may not fit within that particular age range. For example, if your child is a struggling speller, he may fit in the Syllables and Affixes stage according to his age, but his spellings reveal he is in the developmental stage of Within Word Patterns. It is important that you *start teaching at his level of spelling development,* as revealed by his spellings and misspellings.

(2) Your child's movement through the stages may not fit neatly inside just one stage. "Once children begin to use

alphabetic processes, the phases emerge successively. However, unlike stages that are qualitatively distinct, children may use connections from more than one phase. Phases simply characterize the predominant types of alphabetic knowledge used" (Ehri, 2005). A child may be categorized as a Syllable and Affixes speller, but still struggle with a few of the spelling features from the stage before that (Within Word Pattern Speller). It is important that you tailor your spelling instruction to what your child needs. This means you may not want to follow a spelling curriculum a "T." Be sensitive to what your child shows you he needs, based on his spellings and misspellings.

Stage 1: Emergent Spellers

Emergent spellers are anywhere between birth and age 6. Most children that fit in this age have not had any formal lessons on spelling or phonics. They may have observed parents or older siblings as writers and mimic what they see. Children in this age may do some pretend writing. "The children themselves are the only ones who can read what they have written" because, for the most part, the symbols or letters they use are not connected to letter sounds in words (McKenna and Stahl, 2003). Some researchers call this the pre-alphabetic or pre-phonetic stage because most emergent spellers do not understand how letters and their sounds help them spell words, especially in the beginning (Johnston, et. al 2014).

Here are some characteristics of an emergent speller:

Beginning:

- Writing attempts are generally non-alphabetic

- "Spell" haphazardly with marks (such as large scribbles) all over the paper

- Drawing and writing are indistinguishable

Middle:

- Symbols that resemble letters or numbers may be used as they attempt to mimic spelling

- Real letters and numbers may be used, but the speller does not understand that letters represent sounds in words, so *house* may be spelled a1xt

- Prefer writing uppercase letters over lowercase letters

- Begin to write in a linear manner, sometimes left to right

- Drawing and writing begin to become distinguishable

- Do not put space in between words

End:

■ May spell words using the letter names instead of letter sounds (*elephant* may begin with an l because the letter name makes the *el* sound.)

■ Begin to match letters to sounds in words, especially the more prominent sounds. (a word such as *ball* may be spelled with just the letter b, or g for *alligator.*)

■ May confuse letter sounds as they are writing because of the way letters "feel" in the mouth (this relates directly to how spellers pronounce words. For example, the digraph *th* may be spelled with an f.)

■ Tend to confuse letters that have similar sounds or are visually similar (s/c, b, d, p, q)

■ Still tend to prefer writing with uppercase letters, but lower case letters begin to appear

■ Begin to spell some words correctly (such as their name, *mom, cat,* or *love*)

■ Spacing in between words becomes more regular, but can still be random at times

(Bear, et al. 2012 and Johnston, et. al 2014)

Stage 2: Letter Name-Alphabetic Spellers

Letter Name-Alphabetic Spellers range from the time they begin formal instruction in phonics until about the second grade (between 5 and 8 years old). Early in this stage, as kids are taught their letter names, they begin to use the names of the letters to help them spell words. For example, they may associate W with the /d/ sound because the name *double u* starts with /d/. Spellers in this stage typically begin spelling with only consonant sounds because they are more prominent or easier to "feel" in the mouth as the child says the word aloud (Johnston, et al. 2014). As they progress through the stage, they begin to hear more letter sounds (phonemes) in words, including vowel sounds. While we may introduce word family chunks (such as – at in hat, cat, fat, pat, etc.) in our reading instruction, spelling is typically still very much a letter-by-letter production as spellers stretch out the individual sounds in words as they " 'sound their way' through the word to be spelled" (Morris, 2005). Spellers in this stage might also be called semi-phonetic or partial alphabetic because they only represent some of the sounds in words as they write (Johnston, et al. 2014 and Bear, et al. 2012).

Here are some characteristics of letter name - alphabetic speller:

Beginning:

■ Begin to match the written letters in words to letter sounds more consistently, but are still confused by similar sounding letters like f/v, c/s, or k/g

■ Spell words with consonants, very few vowels are used

■ Spell mostly with the beginning and ending sounds (*wall* spelled WL and *heart* spelled HT) or one consonant per syllable (TLFN for *telephone*)

■ Blends are spelled partially (*frog* is spelled with only an F, not an FR)

■ Begin to say words slowly s-t-r-e-t-c-h-i-n-g out the sounds as they write

■ Space in between words becomes even more regular, but can still be lacking at times

■ May still reverse some letters

Middle:

■ Sometimes add vowels in the middle of words, so *bell* may be spelled BAL and *boat* may be BOT (long vowels are easiest to hear and are usually represented first)

■ Say words slowly s-t-r-e-t-c-h-i-n-g out the sounds as they write

■ Begin to hear blends (*fr, gl, sn,* etc.) and represent both sounds, but digraphs (*th, sh, ch, wh)* may still present a bit of trouble because there is only one sound

■ Space in between words is more consistent

■ Begin to spell more high frequency words as reading picks up

End:

■ Begin to spell most short-vowel patterns (CVC) correctly

■ May leave out *n*'s or *m*'s in words (BUP for *bump* or SEG for *sing*)

■ Can spell most consonant blends and digraphs correctly

■ Begin to spell frequently used words correctly as they read more and store words in their memory

■ Still may stretch out individual sounds in words to write them

■ Long vowel words may be spelled incorrectly (WATE for *wait*)

■ Letter reversals are less often, but may still happen on occasion

(Bear, et al. 2012 and Johnston, et. al 2014)

Stage 3: Within Word Pattern Spellers

Spellers in the Within Word Pattern stage begin to "move away from the linear, sound-by-sound approach of the letter name-alphabetic spellers and being to include patterns or chunks of letter sequences" (Bear, et al. 2012). The typical age of a child in this stage is 7 to 10 years old, starting approximately at the end of first grade and ending towards the end of third grade or beginning of fourth grade. In some cases, especially for struggling readers, spellers remain in this stage through middle school.

Here are some characteristics of a within word pattern speller:

■ Begin to correctly spell vowel patterns within one-syllable words, first starting with short vowels and then moving onto long vowels and even some ambiguous vowels.

■ Are comfortable spelling short vowel words with blends and digraphs

18

- Long vowel word patterns may be confused (SOPE for *soap*), but as they progress through this stage, they begin to spell them more conventionally

- Include the *n*'s or *m*'s in words (*bump, sing*)

- R-controlled vowel patterns are spelled correctly (such as *or*, *ar*, or *ir*)

- Misspellings of the ambiguous vowel patterns (such as *ou* or *ei*) may continue

(Bear, et al. 2012)

Stage 4: Syllables and Affixes Spellers

Syllables and Affixes Spellers are typically ages 9 to 14 years and range from the upper elementary grades to middle school. This is the stage where spellers move from spelling patterns in one-syllable words to spelling patterns in multisyllabic words. This is also the stage where students begin to study word meanings, as they study prefixes and suffixes such as *un-* or *pre-*.

Here are some characteristics of a syllables and affixes speller:

- Can spell most one-syllable short, long, and ambiguous words correctly,

■ Confuse spellings where the syllables meet (such as when to double a letter before adding –*ing* or –*ed*), and/or

■ Misspell some prefixes and suffixes (such as PER- for *pre*- or –SION for -*tion*).

(Bear, et al. 2012)

Stage 5: Derivational Relations Spellers

Derivational Relations Spellers begin to connect spelling to meaning, as they focus on taking base words and deriving other words from that base word (for example, *define* to *definition*). Spellers can enter this stage as early as late elementary school, but most spellers in this stage are in middle school, high school, or adults. "The logic inherent in this lifelong stage can be summed up as follows: Words that are related in meaning are often related in spelling as well, despite changes in sound" (Bear, et al. 2012). In other words, if kids understand that words "share the same meaning unit, it is easier for [them] to spell the word correctly" (Hauerwas & Walker, 2004).

While spellers in the derivational relations stage spell common words correctly, they can confuse spellings such as:

■ unaccented syllable spellings (*schwa*), spelling INVUTATION for *invitation*, CONFUDINT for *confident*,

- silent consonants (EMFASIZE for emphasize),

- some suffixes and prefixes (MISPELL for *misspell*),

- related words, so instead of understanding that *favor* and *favorite* share the same base word (*favor*), they base their spellings off the sound, not the meaning, and/or

- "borrowed" word spellings from other languages.

(Bear, et al. 2012)

Chapter 3: Invented Spelling

Before going too much further into spelling instruction, I feel it is necessary to stop and camp for a moment on invented spelling. Invented spelling is one of those topics that I believe is misunderstood among teachers and parents. Just like a child's reading mistakes can help you understand what he knows and what kind of reading instruction he may need, a child's misspellings can do the same for his spelling instruction.

What Is Invented Spelling?

Have you ever noticed that your child makes up or invents the spelling of a word? Maybe she spells *princess* like PRNS or he spells *motorcycle* like MTSKL. This is called invented spelling and it is *directly related* to the level of understanding that your child has about how words and word patterns work (from Chapter 2). If we give children the chance to write independently, we can expect to see invented spelling in their writing because they are still developing an ear for sounds and do not fully understand all the patterns and meaning units of words. But as spellers grow in their knowledge of phonics patterns and sight words and are given systematic and developmentally appropriate spelling instruction, the amount of invented spelling *should* decrease, especially if we hold them accountable to what we have taught them.

Controversy Surrounding Invented Spelling

There is no doubt that invented spelling is surrounded by controversy. Much of this comes from a concern that allowing kids to misspell words sends a message to young writers that it is okay to spell words incorrectly- that spelling does not matter. Some say that by allowing invented spelling, you are teaching young children to become poor spellers. I agree with both of these concerns if invented spelling is the only strategy we teach our writers. If we replace solid spelling instruction with invented spelling, we have failed our writers. If we "let children continue inventing spellings beyond the point where the practice is useful to fulfilling instructional goals" for our youngest learners, we have failed our writers (Stahl, Duffy, Stahl, 1998). As our young spellers become older spellers, we need to be grounding them in an understanding of how words work in a systematic way, teaching them different spelling strategies along the way. You will find suggested spelling strategies for each spelling stage in the next chapter.

Allowing kids to invent spellings "does not mean that [we] do not hold children accountable for accurate spelling. Knowing where children are in terms of development level and considering which word features they have studied enable [us] to set reasonable expectations for accuracy and editing" (Bear et. al,

2012). For example, if your child is a late Letter Name-Alphabetic Speller, it would be unreasonable to expect him to independently spell all long vowel word patterns correctly when he is writing independently. It would be reasonable to expect him to spell most short vowel words (CVC) correctly. The same holds true of the sight words that our kids have and have not studied.

Invented Spelling with Young Writers

Literacy is a developmental process. Babies start learning about literacy through listening to us. After listening and soaking in sounds, they begin to explore and play with those sounds through babbling, making word approximations (dada for daddy), and eventually talking in the conventional sense. Writing and spelling progress much the same way. At first, young writers "babble" their spellings, just like babies babble and explore talking. "When children are first learning to talk, error is not an issue [for parents]. The baby says 'Dadadada' and we wouldn't think of responding, 'Oh, no! He is saying Daddy incorrectly. He isn't ready for whole words, yet.' We do not even regard 'Dadadada' as wrong, but rather an approximation of adult language" (Calkins, 1994). She goes on to ask why we sometimes make such a fuss over these "babbled" spellings.

There are several benefits that come with allowing invented spelling in younger children. When we allow invented spelling in younger children, it makes it easier for them to re-read their own work. This is especially true as writers move into a Letter Name-Alphabetic Speller. Reading their own spelling of ALGATR is typically much easier, developmentally speaking, than reading the conventional spelling (*alligator*) for children in this stage.

Yet another benefit of allowing young writers to invent their spellings is that it stretches their ear to listen for the individual sounds in words (also known as phonemic awareness). In order to invent a spelling, "children need to think about sounds in words and usually do some form of segmentation in order to invent a spelling" (Stahl, Duffy, & Stahl, 1998). What is so important about phonemic awareness? Many early childhood reading researchers identify, "phonemic awareness as one of the most important foundations of reading success" (Yopp & Yopp, 2000). More studies have shown that "first graders who had been encouraged to invent-spell were better at decoding words than first graders from classrooms that emphasized correct spelling" (Cunningham, 2012).

Invented Spelling and Independent Writing

Invented spelling allows children to write down all the creative thoughts in their head. This is especially true in daily journals or

25

as they draft or brainstorm through a topic or story they are writing. Being overly concerned about spelling can prevent some writers, especially young writers and/or reluctant writers, from being creative in their writing because they feel they must stick to writing words they already know how to spell.

Invented Spelling Benefits the Teacher

As mentioned in Chapter 1, invented spelling gives you a little "window" into what your child does and does not fully understand about word features and patterns. Just like analyzing your child's reading mistakes is an important step into figuring out what kind of reading instruction he may need, analyzing your child's invented spellings is an important part of guiding your spelling instruction. Later in this chapter, we will talk more about how to analyze your child's misspellings.

Common Questions about Invented Spelling

How do you know when to ask your child to give you more with his spellings?

What your child can/cannot spell varies from each developmental stage to the next as he grows in his knowledge of spelling patterns and spelling strategies. In order to know what to expect from your child (and when to push for more), you need to have a general idea of his level of spelling development. For example, a child spells FOG for *frog* (missing the *r* in the blend). If the child is not at a level of sound awareness to hear the two individual sounds in the blend, requiring him to independently spell *frog* in a conventional way would be absurd. Asking more of a speller when he is not ready frustrates him; it is like taking the training wheels off before the child is ready to ride his bike. On the other hand, if he is developmentally ready for blends and/or we have worked on blends in his spelling instruction, he should be challenged to listen for the blend and asked to write both sounds. *Please note that we can and should model spelling concepts that are developmentally "over his head" for our young speller. (We do this all the time when we read aloud to children.) In the specific case mentioned above, the adult can model how to stretch the word out slowly and help the child hear both sounds by over-emphasizing both the* f *and* r. *After modeling it, ask the speller to correct his spelling to include both the* f *and* r.

When should you correct a child's invented spellings/misspellings?

If your child has been taught it, hold him accountable. Accountability for correct spelling should start on day one. "Children (and adults also) will always invent a spelling for what they do not yet know," but if they do know it, hold them accountable (Bear, et al. 2012).

When a child is writing a text that will be re-read often by them and/or others (such as a poem or story he "publishes"), it is important that the words are spelled correctly. This does not always mean that we should make a big "to do" about every invented spelling. If a child as gone through the drafting, revising, and editing stage of writing and corrected all the words for which he has strategies, the rest of the editing can be accomplished without the need to make a "teachable moment" out of all the other misspelled words. Simply scratch out the invented spelling and spell the word conventionally above it.

Let's face it: conventional spelling is a courtesy to the reader. While grandparents and the occasional friendly neighbor may enjoy a letter from our young writer adorned with invented spellings (After all, some invented spellings are simply adorable.), we need to help older writers realize that conventional spelling does matter to the reader. Taking the time to correct those misspellings shows the reader that we really do care.

Your child may begin to ask such questions as: "Did I spell this word right?" or "How do you spell fill in the blank?" There are many ways to handle these questions about spelling and it all

28

depends on several possibilities such as: Does the child possess the strategies and knowledge to spell the word? Can I stop what I am doing to help the child right now or am I working with another child? What is the purpose of the child's writing?

If you are working with the child as he writes *and the word in question has spelling patterns or features that are too difficult for him*, help him spell the word. If you are working with another child or cannot attend to the spelling issue right away, ask the child to go ahead and try his best with the word. Once he has spelled it to the best of his ability, ask him to circle or underline it lightly. This is a signal to the child and to you that the word may not be spelled conventionally. As soon as you can, attend to the word and help the child spell it. Encourage the child to spell the word in question by himself so that he can move on to the next part of his sentence or thoughts. The purpose of independent writing time is to write; to get meaning and thoughts on paper. We do not want our writers to sit and waste ten minutes of energy and time on spelling one word.

If the child asks how to spell a word *and you know that he possesses the spelling knowledge to spell it correctly, do not spell the word for him right away.* Instead, give spelling strategy hints. For example, if he asks me to spell *treat*, say something like, "Well, I hear the word *eat* in that word. How do you spell *eat*? You can use *eat* to help you spell *treat*." We want our spellers to understand that we are not his only resource, that there are other spelling strategies that can help him spell words. It is important to understand that as spellers progress in their awareness of words, they will begin to recognize when a word they have written is spelled incorrectly. This is a good thing! "Many [spellers] who use inventive spelling know that the incorrectly spelled word *looks* wrong. We want them to be able to recognize incorrect spelling in their own writing, and rewrite the word correctly" (http://bit.ly/1g28Tx7). We will talk more about effective spelling strategies in the next chapter.

Should invented spelling be allowed with older writers...ever?

My answer is "yes," but with *lots* of limits. The two specific times that I allow invented spelling with older children are (1) during their independent writing time (such as writing in a journal) and (2) when they are in brainstorming mode and the writer's message and ideas are desired over spelling. For example, creative, independent writing time should be a judge-free zone. When a child is writing an impromptu "I love you" note to his daddy or writing in his journal, I do not recommend critiquing his every spelling. While spelling errors can be pointed out at times, the message is the focus, not his misspellings.

This is also true when he is in brainstorm mode or getting his thoughts down before writing. While this is a fine line, if a writer wants to brainstorm alone, do not expect that every single word will be conventionally spelled. And, while we emphasize how important correct spelling is any time we write, we do not want him to be so consumed with spelling every word correctly that the message he seeks to get down on paper is compromised. Stopping to work on spelling strategies for every single word he needs to spell or misspells as he is brainstorming (or writing a rough draft) can greatly hinder his message, much like stopping continually to talk about word patterns in "tricky" words in the middle of reading a text.

If your older child is brainstorming alone, here are a few ideas that can him with spelling. Encourage him to use his resources (from his spelling instruction). If he is writing about a topic such as trains and you have a book about trains nearby, he can use the book to help him find and spell words conventionally. Brainstorm words he may need to use in his writing ahead of time together. Jot those words down on a dry erase board or paper so he can have them as a resource. If he comes to a word that he simply does not have all the strategies for, he can ask for help or he can invent the spelling, using all the strategies he has been taught to the best of his abilities. When a child does this, ask him to lightly circle or underline because you want to see if

31

he can recognize his misspellings. Note that when brainstorming or drafting mode is over and editing time comes, we take time to look at all his misspellings. This is when we work on spelling strategies for some of the misspelled words. For other words (those he does not have the strategies to spell), simply spell the word for him.

Will allowing a child to invent a spelling hinder correct spelling?

If invented spelling is the main strategy we teach spellers, no matter their age, then yes. If invented spelling is used in place of teaching phonics and sight words, then yes. If we do not hold our kids accountable for what we have taught them, then yes. But if we use invented spelling as just one strategy to help spellers work independently by spelling words they have not yet mastered, then no. Literacy works best when it is approached in a balanced way. To say that spellers can never use invented spelling is unreasonable. Even adults do at times.

One last word on invented spelling: Invented spelling does not *replace* solid spelling instruction. But if used as a diagnostic tool, invented spelling can help you *place* your solid spelling instruction at the right level for your speller. The next few sections will explain more about doing just this.

Determining Your Child's Level of Spelling Development

The question lingers after all this talk about spelling development: How do I know the level of my child's spelling development? After all, this is the level your child's spelling instruction needs to teach to. There are a couple ways to figure it out. (1) You can give your child a spelling inventory (like a spelling test) and/or (2) observe him as he writes independently.

Spelling Inventories

One way that you can get a snap shot of your child's spelling development (from Chapter 2) is to administer a spelling inventory. A spelling inventory allows you to quickly see a child's strengths and weaknesses concerning his spelling and phonics knowledge. The words on the inventories are specifically chosen to display a student's knowledge and understanding of certain spelling features (short vowels, long vowels, blends, etc.) The words begin at a rather "easy" level and gradually become more difficult to spell. This assessment is administered in a similar fashion as a spelling test, except students have not studied these specific words beforehand. When giving a spelling inventory to your child, allow for 10 to 20 minutes to administer it. Once the inventory has been taken, you can analyze your child's spellings to find the level of spelling development that best fits him. This is where your spelling instruction should begin.

The researchers and writers of Words Their Way have developed three spelling inventories, depending on the age of your child. The Primary Spelling Inventory is designed for spellers in the Emergent to Within Word Pattern Speller range (approximately grades K-3). The Elementary Spelling Inventory is designed for late Letter Name-Alphabetic spellers to early Derivational Relations Spellers (approximately grades 1-6). And the Upper-Level Spelling Inventory is designed for Within Word Pattern to Derivational Relations Spellers (approximately grades 5-12). You can find all these spelling inventories as well as clear directions on how to analyze the results Words Their Way (http://amzn.to/OeDhyo).

You can also find an example of how I did this with my own child at my website, This Reading Mama (http://bit.ly/1cXsgYe).

Analyzing Your Child's Spellings in the Context of Writing

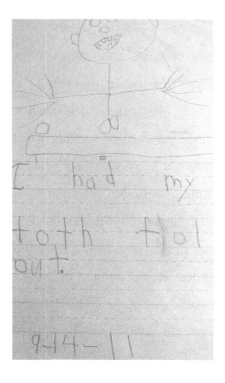

Aside from giving your child a spelling inventory, it is also helpful to look at a child's spellings from his independent writing. "An analysis of several work samples is often helpful to assess children's knowledge of spelling patterns. Such analysis allows [you] to determine which patterns the child does not know" (Hauerwas & Walker, 2004). If you help your child write, note the kinds of patterns and features he asks assistance to spell. If he writes independently, maybe in a notebook or journal, take the time to revisit his independent writing without him. As you look over his writing, note the spellings he demonstrates an understanding of and what he invent-spells.

The appendix has a printable chart you can use as you analyze your child's spellings. Listed in the second column are word features to look for in his writings. The chart will help you note if he has a clear understanding of spelling words with that word feature or if he does not yet possess a clear understanding. Start with the first feature (beginning consonants). If your child has spelled all of his beginning consonants correctly in his writing, check off "Demonstrates a Clear Understanding." Continue going down the word feature column in this manner. When you get to a word feature in which your child misspells two or more of that feature in his writing, check, "Not a Complete Understanding." In the right-hand column (labeled "Notes"), jot down his misspellings from that word feature. For example, if he spelled SOPE for *soap* and WATE for *wait*, write the way he misspelled those words in your "Notes" column.

The word features in this checklist continue to become more complex. Once you have checked, "Not a Complete Understanding" for a word feature, chances are the next couple on the list will also be checked, "Not a Complete Understanding." Instead of stopping after the first time you have checked in this column, return to his writing and analyze it for a couple more word features, just to be sure you are collecting enough information.

Once you have three checks in the column, "Not a Complete Understanding", stop. Return to the first word feature for which you checked, "Not a Complete Understanding." For our example above, the first check would be in Long Vowel Patterns. Listed in the far left-hand column are the spelling stages we examined in Chapter 2 (Emergent, Letter Name-Alphabet, Within Word Pattern, Syllables and Affixes, and Derivational Relations.) Each of the spelling features correlates with one of these spelling stages. In the example of the child misspelling the long vowel patterns, he would be developmentally ready for more spelling strategies for a Within Word Pattern Speller.

Please note that this is an informal way of assessing your child's spellings. If you are unsure of your estimation, based on your analysis, ask someone else to analyze it as well. Also note that there may be times when one particular spelling feature is not evident in your child's writing. For example, he may not have used any digraphs. When this happens, just write "N/O" (for "not observed") in the "Notes" column.

Spelling Instruction Level for Struggling Spellers

Some children benefit from going back (or down) a spelling level in instruction at first. This is particularly true of struggling readers and spellers. *All About Spelling* suggests doing this, because there may be "holes in his knowledge of spelling" that need to be filled in with some review first. "You can move as quickly or as slowly as your student needs. If you are working with an older student, he probably understands some of the concepts but not others. In this case, very quickly skim the parts that he already knows and slow down on the parts that he needs to learn" (http://www.allaboutlearningpress.com/which-spelling-level-should-we-start-with).

Struggling spellers may also struggle a bit with motivation, especially if they have been operating with spelling instruction that has been on their frustration level. Going down one level may help build back the motivation needed. (If you have an older struggling speller, you may want to read *All About Spelling*'s post on using their curriculum with older spellers at http://bit.ly/1isklpr.)

Chapter 4: Developmental Spelling Strategies

When teaching a beginning reader, we focus on reading strategies to help him figure out (or decode) unknown words. We may say things like, "sound it out" or "look at the picture to help you figure out the word." But as readers grow in their knowledge of how words work, they begin to outgrow these initial strategies. Some of the strategies that worked as a beginning reader no longer sustain them as the texts get longer and words become more difficult. What do we do then? We teach them new strategies, of course! What does this have to do with spelling? Absolutely everything!

When teaching a beginning writer/speller (Preschool or Kindergartner), we also zero in on a few strategies that will help them when they write. One very common strategy for beginning writers is invented spelling (see Chapter 3). In this stage of development, before they have a full knowledge of how sounds and patterns work in spelling, invented spelling is one of the main spelling strategies they use. But as spellers begin to understand how sounds and words work (through the teaching of phonics and spelling patterns), they need to move on to more reliable spelling strategies. Just like the "sound it out" strategy with reading will become a hindrance for older readers, invented spelling will become a hindrance for older spellers. (But note that even adults still use invented spelling from time to time!)

39

In this chapter, we will talk about spelling strategies for each level of spelling development from Chapter 2. Please note that while these spelling strategies are suggested in these specific stages, good spellers use a mix of different strategies as they spell. Just because the strategy is not mentioned until a later spelling stage does not mean we have to wait to model it for our child. For example, even preschoolers can begin to understand that prefixes have meaning; that *triceratops*, *tricycle*, and *triangle* all start with *tri-*, which means three.

Beginning Spellers (Emergent)

Beginning spellers, specifically those in the beginning- to middle-emergent stage, do not typically have a concept of letters, much less how letters and sounds dance together to spell words. Some would argue that children at this age should not be encouraged (or even allowed) to write. I would have to say I agree wholeheartedly with Lucy Calkins when she says, "It is not children but adults who have separated writing from art, song, and play; it is adults who have turned writing into an exercise on lined paper, into a matter of rules, lessons, and cautious behavior. We, as adults, may not believe in writing for preschool children—but the children believe in it" (Calkins, 59).

From a young age, we need to allow our children to explore and play with writing. Just like we encourage our toddlers to talk,

40

even though they cannot do it conventionally just yet, we need to encourage our little ones to write and "spell," even if it is not in a conventional manner. We must be willing "to stretch the boundaries of what counts as…writing behavior" (Schickedanz et al, 1990).

The best strategy for spellers in this stage is exploration. Much of a child's writing at this age is based on drawing pictures and making scribbles. We must provide writing opportunities that are play-based and simply let them explore writing. Think markers, crayons, and sidewalk chalk; think blank paper, chalkboards, and dry erase boards. If you want mess-free play, there are plenty of no-mess writing products on the market, providing wonderful invitations for kids to explore writing (You can see a list of my favorites in the No-Mess Section in Chapter 8.) Model writing for him. Let him see you write that grocery list. Make letter sounds out loud as you write so he can hear you modeling the connection between the spoken word and the written word. Invite and encourage him to "write" his own list beside you as he scribbles along. Show him how to write and spell his own name, which is one of the most important words he will learn to read (and possibly write) at this stage. But above all, treat his writing as important. Respect what he has to "say" and invite him to share it with you.

In this stage, we should also introduce letters and their sounds to students. But as we do, we want to split up instruction of letter sounds that are similar. For example, introducing the sound of *b* and *p* at the same time would serve to confuse a child in this stage because both of their sounds are created by placing the two lips together. Marie Rippel, of *All About Spelling* (http://bit.ly/1cKezBJ) also warns against introducing the vowel sounds at the same time (Rippel, 2013). Listening for beginning sounds is the most developmentally appropriate place to start for a child in this spelling stage. When we do, we may want to elongate, exaggerate or repeat the beginning sound so the child can better hear the sound. Another strategy to use with spellers of this stage when learning letter sounds in words is to have the child say the word with you so he can "feel" the sounds in his mouth.

Letter Name-Alphabetic Spellers

As children begin to learn their letters and letter sounds, they start to connect the two as they spell (phonics). While these connections are growing, spellers in this stage still do not have a full understanding of the alphabet. The strategy they naturally tend to use when spelling is the "sound it out" approach, or invented spelling (see Chapter 3). In this spelling stage, invented spelling is not only allowed, it is encouraged. Why? "Children who are allowed and encouraged to 'invent-spell' develop an early and strong sense of phonemic awareness" (Cunningham, 26). Phonemic awareness, the ability to hear individual sounds in words, is an early predictor of reading and without it "the symbol system [for reading and writing] is arbitrary. The task of dealing with the symbol system...can quickly become overwhelming" (Yopp & Yopp, 2000). Not only that, but if we always require conventional spelling at this level of letter and sound understanding, the spelling strategy we inadvertently teach spellers is "ask an adult." In doing so, spellers can become reliant on our spelling strategies instead of developing their own.

Spellers in this stage should be explicitly taught how to listen for sounds in words and write down the sounds they hear. It does not matter so much that they get every letter-sound relationship correct, especially at first. "The important thing for now is that we and our children realize that once they know a handful of sound-symbol correspondences, they can write anything they wish." (Calkins, 1994). As they develop an ear for letter sounds and learn that their print has meaning to them and to others, our job is to celebrate their spellings and their message, not condemn them for misspelling words.

Model how to listen for sounds in words by stretching out the word slowly. Tell them that you can stretch words out like a rubber band. Say the word slowly and invite the child to write down the individual sounds he hears. As mentioned in Chapter 2, children's spellings in this stage reveal that they do "pay attention to physical sensations when they try to spell" (Johnston, et al. 2014). Kids typically only write down the most salient sounds in a word. And when they do not have a full understanding of letter sounds, they may "use the names of the letters as cues to the sounds they want to represent." For example, the letter Y may represent a /w/ sound as the letter Y's name begins with the /w/ sound (Bear, et al. 2012).

"The fact that we watch and celebrate what children can do doesn't mean that we necessarily maintain a hands-off policy when our kids write. It does mean that our teaching is in response to what children do" (Calkins, 1994). As we teach letter sounds and the speller's knowledge of them grows, we challenge the young speller to listen for more sounds. While he may only spell BL for *ball*, we ask him to listen for a sound in between those two sounds. Spellers "should be taught to…listen for each sound in a word and to represent each sound with a letter or combination of letters." These sounds the speller can hear should be represented in their spellings (http://bit.ly/1ndN8Va). From the start, we must hold kids accountable for what they know about spelling, even if it still does not create a conventional spelling.

Invented spelling, even at this stage, does *not* completely replace conventional spelling. As a speller's knowledge of sounds grows, his ability to remember sight words (see Chapter 5) also expands. As early sight words (also sometimes referred to as high frequency words) are taught, we should place them in a prominent place so he can remember the conventional spelling. The sight words we have taught spellers are not words we want kids to invent-spell. As kids are taught these words, we hold them accountable for spelling them conventionally.

As we expect spellers to write down letters and get meaning on paper, handwriting instruction is also needed at this level of development. This is because a lack of handwriting knowledge can distract kids from remembering and getting their message onto the paper. Instead of using handwriting worksheets, teach handwriting in fun ways, using some of the same writing tools that were used in the emergent stage of spelling. Another effective way to teach handwriting is in the context of real writing. As you work beside the child, you can provide helpful hints and reminders that certain letters need to be capital and others do not. In this stage, there is still a large handwriting curve when it comes to independent writing time. Some letters may still get confused (such as *b* and *d*) and random capital letters may appear. In these cases, I praise the child for what he has done in his writing and provide instruction when needed.

Sometimes, I do not correct the handwriting mistakes immediately, but store them away for a later time of instruction.

In this stage, modeling your life as a speller is highly important. Tackle spelling tasks together. After your child has drawn a picture, work on writing the sentence together (shared writing). Shared writing, or interactive writing, is a highly effective way to work on many writing skills, including spelling. To share the writing, you need to know what your child can and cannot do in regards to handwriting and spellings as well as things he needs to practice more. You will want to have resources within your reach such as a handwriting chart (to show correct letter formation), a letter sounds chart, and/or a list of the sight words your child can spell (see resources in the appendix). While writing a sentence together, you can write parts of it that may be too hard for your child and your child writes other parts that are attainable for him. For example, if your child has learned *the*, ask him to write *the* in the sentence. Shared writing can be a time when you explore the sounds in words together or a time of modeling handwriting or conventional spelling. The possibilities of shared writing are almost endless.

Within Word Pattern Spellers

When kids reach the Within Word Pattern stage, some exciting changes happen. One of the biggest changes is the gradual

46

abandonment of the sound-by-sound spelling that they have used in the last two stages of spelling. Starting in this stage, spellers begin to understand that "sound and pattern [work] simultaneously" and that they can spell words using common patterns. For example, *cat* can help them spell *flat* because they both contain the –*at* chunk (Bear, et al. 2012). While spellers in the Letter Name-Alphabetic stage may begin using word families to read, writers in this stage begin to use them to spell words. This is a powerful tool because learning to spell with word chunks, or word families, can help spellers write "thousands of words in which these word families regularly appear. For example, the rime -*am* can help with words like *ham, Sam, slam,* and *jam* [as well as longer words like] *Abraham, Amsterdam, bedlam, camera, hamster, grammar, telegram,* and many more" (Rasinki, Rupley & Nichols, 2008). Just how effective are word family chunks in spelling? In 1970, two reading researchers published 37 rimes (or word family chunks) that could help kids spell 500 words. Another researcher (Fry) published that 30 word family chunks can create a whopping 654 one-syllable words in the English language! (Johnston, 67)

Included in the appendix are some common word family patterns that can help your child spell (and read) a plethora of words. Word families are most effective when children first start with the short and long vowels patterns. As they begin to move deeper into the short and long vowel patterns, comparing multiple word family patterns at the same time helps to expand spellers' understanding of how to use these patterns in their own spellings. Shifting the focus to word chunks or patterns is beneficial for spellers as their awareness of short and long vowel patterns continues to grow further. For example, instead of comparing word families, demonstrate how to use the chunk (or phonogram) of *ai* to spell other words that contain *ai* (like *rain*, *braid*, and *paint*). The Short, Long, and Other Vowel Patterns chart in the appendix lists some common vowel patterns for this stage.

Aside from the fact that kids can read and spell many words based on patterns, brain research confirms the use of patterns in spelling instruction. "Brain research suggests that the brain is a pattern detector, not a rule applier and that, while we look at single letters, we are looking at them and considering all the letter patterns we know. Successfully decoding [or spelling] a word occurs when the brain recognizes a familiar spelling pattern, or if the pattern itself is not familiar, the brain searches through its store of words with similar patterns" (Cunningham, 2005). Spelling words by pattern (also known as spelling words by analogy) will not only serve the child well in this stage, but also throughout life as a speller.

Another exciting change in this stage is that a child's sight word recognition also expands greatly, as he is able to "hook" the new words onto his solid foundation of letter sounds (phonemes) and word patterns. Teachers of spellers in this stage should take advantage of the opportunity to connect these sight words with spelling patterns. "For example, the word *see* can be used to teach students the double *ee* spelling of the long *e* vowel, and it is generative in the sense that students can use it to help spell a host of words with *-ee, -eed, -eek, -eel, -eem, -een, -eep, -eet,* and *-eeze* endings (e.g., *tree, feed, week, wheel, seem, green, sheep, beet, sneeze*)" (Williams et al. 2009).

In this stage of spelling development, reading begins to become more independent, as children in this stage have a "sizable growth in their sight vocabularies as a result of reading practice" and new decoding strategies (Ehri, 1999). If we expose our kids to texts that are appropriate (http://bit.ly/1iuoZaA) and continue working on common sight words and spelling by analogy, the way is paved for yet another highly effective spelling strategy: visualizing words. We need to teach kids to think about how a word looks in their head. Have they seen the word in print? And when they spell the word, they can ask themselves "does the word look right? Good spellers often try spelling a word several ways to see which way looks correct" (http://bit.ly/1ndN8Va). In the appendix, you will find a "Try It! Page" that can help spellers do just this. Using the first two columns, encourage the speller to try the word two different ways. Once he has attempted the word and if it still does not look right, he is encouraged to bring the paper to you, as the teacher. In the third column, you write the word conventionally. Your child's "Try It! Page" can serve as a make-shift dictionary as he may need to spell some of the same words on another occasion.

In this stage of spelling, we can teach spellers yet another useful strategy- using multiple kinds of resources to look up words if they are unsure of spellings. Providing spellers with a kid-friendly spelling dictionary is a great place to start. While we may model how to use various resources in the stages that come before this one, using a kid-friendly spelling dictionary begins to be more effective starting in this stage. Why? Because kids' invented spellings in this stage begin to better align with conventional spellings, making it easier to look up a word. After all, in order to find a word in a dictionary, you need to know how to spell it! Providing a way to record sight words or words you have studied is also a great way to provide spelling resources for your child. You can read more about this in the last section of this chapter or in Chapter 5.

Syllables and Affix Spellers and Derivational Relation Spellers

As spellers come into the Syllable and Affix stage, they begin to move into spelling words with more than one syllable. Beginning in this stage, we also add another spelling strategy: using word meanings to help with spelling. This continues even into the Derivational Relation Speller stage. In these stages, spellers learn words "according to spelling, meaning, and patterns in order to better understand how spelling represents a word's meaning and grammatical function" (Invernizzi, Abouzeid, & Bloodgood, 1997). For example, in the Syllables and Affixes stage, we may help spellers see the relationship between the final spelling of – or, -ar, and –er and the way these endings have grammar connections (Invernizzi, Abouzeid, & Bloodgood, 1997). These meaning "strategies are based on the knowledge of how the meaning of a word influences its spelling. We should be teaching Greek and Latin roots and words based on other derivatives, how to add prefixes and suffixes to base words, and how to form compound words and abbreviations"(http://bit.ly/1ndN8Va).

Included in the appendix are some common syllable juncture and derivational relations spelling patterns, prefixes, suffixes, roots, and base words for these stages. My list is by no means exhaustive. Levels 6 and 7 of *All About Spelling* have several lessons that correlate with these features. Appendix E in *Words Their Way* has a thorough list of these patterns and word meanings.

Developmental Spelling Strategies

Emergent Spellers

- Simply explore writing in a playful way

- Provide opportunities for "spelling" and writing

- Encourage independent writing time

- Verbally call their scribbles "writing"

- Begin introducing beginning letter sounds by elongating, exaggerating, or repeating the first sound in words

- Ask the child to say the word out loud so he can "feel" how his mouth makes particular letter sounds

- Teach a few important words, like their name

Letter Name-Alphabet Spellers

- Work on handwriting in hands-on and fun ways (worksheets should not be your child's main diet!)

- Listen for sounds in words and write down the sounds you hear

- Allow invented spelling, but hold kids accountable for what you have taught them and what they know about letter sounds

Developmental Spelling Strategies

- Share the pen, asking kids to do what they can as you write together

- Begin learning basic sight words at a slow pace and start a dictionary together

Within Word Alphabet Spellers

- Continue to allow invented spelling during independent writing time, but help spellers see that the following spelling strategies are highly effective in spelling unknown words

- Begin to focus on word families and word patterns as a means to spelling unknown words

- Continue teaching sight words and hold kids accountable to the words you have studied

- Use a basic or beginner spelling dictionary (based on word families, word patterns, or sight words you have studied)

- Provide a way to record sight words studied (such as a Word Wall)

- Help them visualize words as they have seen them in their reading. Ask, "Does my spelling look right?"

Developmental Spelling Strategies

Syllable and Affix Spellers & Derivational Relation Spellers

■ Continue in the teaching of sight words

■ Study how words are put together, especially in words with more than one syllable

■ Begin making spelling-meaning connections, as words that share similar meanings usually share similar spellings (example: *differ* and *different*)

■ Begin making spelling-grammar connections, as many words are spelled according to their grammatical usage

■ Learn and study Greek root and Latin stem origins to words and how those affect the spellings of words

Resources for Holding Kids Accountable

In all of this, we should be holding spellers accountable from the beginning for what they know. In the appendix, you will find several resources that can help you do this with your spellers.

Beginning Letter Sound Chart- As children learn letter sounds, this chart can be used. For example, if a child needs to spell a word such as *fox*, you can point him to the letter sounds within the chart that can help him spell the word.

Letter Blends/Digraphs- As spellers move into the end of the Letter Name-Alphabetic stage, they are better able to listen for blends and digraphs. If a child needs to spell *flop*, you can say something like, "Look on the chart. There is a word that starts just like *flop*. Can you find it and use it to help you spell the sounds at the beginning of *flop*?"

Word Family Dictionary*- Once a child begins to study patterns within words, which can start in the late-Letter Name-Alphabetic stage, begin recording the word families you study on these pages. On each page, write one word family you are working on (for example, *-an*). On the lines provided, ask your child to write *–an* words you find in your reading or work on during spelling. The list you create will probably take more than one sitting. For example, if your child comes across the word *candy* in reading, you could make a big deal by saying, "Oh, this word contains the *–an* family. Let's use the *–an* family to help us read it. Now, let's write it on our *–an* page!"

Word Pattern Dictionary*- When children move into the Within Word Pattern Stage, they can begin to use those patterns (or chunks) to help them read and spell new words. On each page, write one spelling pattern you are working on (for example o_e). On the lines provided, ask your child to write words you find in your reading and work on during spelling that contain this specific word pattern. Continue collecting words from your reading and writing time. This can be used during independent writing time as a resource for different spelling patterns.

*Both the Word Family Dictionary and Word Pattern Dictionary can be printed off many times and put together in a notebook or stapled together to make a book containing different phonics patterns. The cover pages are included for both kinds of dictionaries in the appendix.

Common Vowel Patterns in One-Syllable Words- Even after spellers "exit" the Within Word Pattern stage, they may still confuse spelling patterns that sound the same (such as *o_e*, *oa*, *ow*, and *oe* for long *o*). Keep this one-page chart close by for independent writing time. It is also a great resource when spellers ask, "How do you spell *clown*?" You can refer to the chart and say something like, "It has the same spelling pattern as *cow.*"

Chapter 5: Spelling Sight Words

Sight words truly are any words that a child recognizes by sight. Included among these words may be their own name or other important words, such as *mom* or *dad* (McKenna & Stahl, 2003). For our purposes, we will refer to sight words as words that occur frequently as children read and write (also referred to as high frequency words): words such as *the*, *you*, or *can*. Why are sight words so important? Because these words are so frequently used in the English language that we want them to become automatic for our kids in their reading and in their spelling. This means our readers and spellers can interact with these words without needing to spend so much brain power on them. Freeing the brain from using its energy on common sight words helps our readers focus more on comprehension as they read and helps our spellers focus more on getting their message down on paper as they write. In this chapter, we will talk a little more spelling sight words and how these words fit into spelling development.

What Sight Words do I Teach?

There are many different lists for sight words or high frequency words. The two most common lists are the Dolch word lists and Fry's list of high frequency words. *I prefer Fry's list over the Dolch list for many reasons, mostly because the Dolch list has words listed at a third grade level that children can most definitely learn earlier, as compared to their letter and sound knowledge (such as* if, six, *and* got*)*. Because of copyright laws, I am unable to provide these lists in my book. To locate them, simply type in the name of each list into your favorite internet search engine and you will be sure to find them. (Florida Center for Reading Research (http://www.fcrr.org/index.shtml) has high frequency lists for students under Student Center Activities (http://www.fcrr.org/curriculum/SCAindex.shtm), formed from what seems to be a combination of Dolch words and Fry's words). The most important thing you are looking for as you look at word lists is that the words first listed are the highest in frequency (words like *the*, *I* or *and*). This is where instruction with high frequency needs to begin.

How do I Help Sight Words to "Stick" in Memory?

Understanding your child's spelling development (from Chapter 2) can also help you know how and when to introduce spelling sight words. In Ehri & McCormick's article, *Phases of Word Learning*, they create some developmentally sound arguments for how kids learn sight words.

In the Emergent stage, spellers have a very limited knowledge of letters. They also do not understand the connection between letters and their sounds, as demonstrated in their scribbles and drawings. In this phase of learning, kids may be able to "read" a few words, mostly environmental print (like the sign of a store or favorite cereal box). They may even be able to remember a few words because of their shape, such as the *oo*'s in *look*, acting as two eyes looking. But because kids lack a knowledge of how letters and sounds work, they do not connect these words to letters or sounds, but rather their shape or "picture." The problem with remembering words by their shape/picture is that there simply isn't enough of a visual difference between words for the child to even have a chance! For example, when the child is faced with *took*, she will probably say it is *look* because *took* also has *oo*'s in the middle that look like eyes. *Big* (because of its tail) may also be read *dog*. Ehri suggests that some readers may even say *see* for *look* because they can't read the actual word, so their strategy is to remember the concept of the word (Ehri & McCormick, 1999). In the Emergent stage of spelling, we most certainly can begin teaching spellers the letters in their name. But beyond that, spelling sight words, or other words, will be very difficult because the child lacks the alphabetic understanding.

As your child moves into the Letter Name-Alphabetic stage, he begins to develop letter sense; that letters correspond with sounds. In this stage, you can more successfully begin introducing sight words to your speller. But because children in this stage still lack the ability to crack the code of letter sounds completely, "they process only partial-letter relations to form connections in learning sight words." (Ehri & McCormick, 1999). Sight words can be learned in this stage, but separately teaching similarly spelled sight words is key. For example, words like *no* and *on* should be taught at separate times to limit confusion. It is also important to introduce sight words at a slow pace, such as the pace found in my *Reading the Alphabet* curriculum (http://bit.ly/1lqywNm).

When spellers grow into the Within Word Pattern stage, they are said to be full-alphabetic spellers, meaning they can understand and process letter-sound correspondences, including vowels and other phonogram sets like *ch* or *th*. As kids "acquire sufficient knowledge of the alphabetic system, they are able to learn sight words quickly and to remember them long term" (Ehri, 2005). This is also the stage at which we spellers beginning to question their misspellings more.

Tricky Sight Words

While sight word (or high frequency word) memory may begin to blossom in the Within Word Pattern stage, some sight words are just tricky. Many of these words are the ones that break those phonics rules and generalizations we try to teach. What can we do with these sight words? A few suggestions are:

■ Tie in phonics. For example, a word like *not* can be decoded in a letter-by-letter way (/n/-/o/-/t/), while sight words like *night* contain word family chunks (–ight) and/or word patterns (igh=long i), helping readers spell other words. Instead of studying sight words separately, help spellers see the connection they have to their phonics knowledge. Some sight words can be taught out of their suggested order. For example, on the third grade Dolch list, you will find *if* and *six*. I like to teach these at the same time that I teach the short *i* sound in words (well before third grade!). Tying in phonics instruction helps spellers have more than just one way of organizing words in their heads, making words easier to remember.

■ Compare the tricky word with other words like it. This is what *Words Their Way* (http://amzn.to/OeDhyo) does. When a sight word fits within a particular category in a sort, it is included in the sort and is sorted just like the rest of the words (such as *like*). Sometimes the sight word is an exception to the rule or generalization (like *said*). By comparing the sight words along with the phonics words, we are building a strong connection to that sight word.

■ Acknowledge and talk about the tricky parts of the word. What parts are "easy" and what parts are "tricky." For example, while examining the word *they*, ask questions like, "What part of this word is the easiest part to spell?" and "What part of this word is the trickiest part for you?" Follow up with "Why?" Talking explicitly about words and their tricky parts helps our kids to slow down and really focus on the spelling. This can help them remember the spelling better.

■ Display highly used sight words, even if you have not introduced them in your spelling instruction. The word *because* is a perfect example of this. When my son was in Kindergarten, he would quite often ask me, "How do you spell *because*?" We had not studied this particular word in his sight word work, but because he needed it so much, I placed it on our word wall. I took it a step further and placed it directly on his school desk so he could see it. I did the same thing with the word *favorite* towards the end of Kindergarten.

■ Create mnemonics (or visual pictures) for those words that are particularly tricky. *Sight Words You Can See* (http://www.readingwithtlc.com/site-words.html)   from *Reading with TLC* has done just this. This program was created to help kids "link the way a word is printed to the way it should be pronounced, and even better, to its meaning" (http://bit.ly/1crioep).

As spellers begin to grow into studying the meaning of words, it can be interesting to also study the origin of words. Sometimes the origin of the word dictates its spelling, such as the word *beautiful.* This is why you often hear kids in a national spelling bee ask what the origin of a word is. Sites like Online Etymology Dictionary (http://www.etymonline.com/) can be a great resource for kids to study origins of words.

Holding Kids Accountable with Sight Words

Just like we must hold kids accountable for spelling phonics patterns we have taught them, we must also hold them accountable to spelling the sight words they have been taught correctly. Two great ways to do this are:

Create a word wall (http://thisreadingmama.com/2013/05/22/the-teaching-of-sight-words-part-2/) or some kind of record chart that lists alphabetically which words you and your child have studied together. All the sight words starting with the letter *a* would go under a column or in a space labeled *a*, those starting with *b* would go under *b*, etc. Keeping a word wall does occupy a lot of space. Using a manila folder like the one you see pictured above to record alphabetically the sight words your child has studied can be more compact and portable.

The important thing with keeping a recorded chart or word wall is that you remove words once your child has shown he can spell them independently and replace them with new words. For example, the sight word *the* did not stay on my son's word wall that long. Because he read and spelled that word quite frequently, he had lots of meaningful exposure to the word. It did not take much time for him to internalize the spelling. Once I noticed that he no longer referred to his word wall to spell *the*, I removed it. There are other words that have been on his word wall (or folder) longer because they are less frequent and have not been completely moved into memory.

Use a spelling dictionary. In the appendix, I have included a spelling dictionary template for the sight words you and your child study. In the box, write a letter of the alphabet. In the blank spaces provided, ask your child to record the sight words you teach your child that begin with that specific letter. Print off a page for each letter of the alphabet, although you may be able to combine letters like *x* and *y* on one page, a Spelling Dictionary cover page, and place them in a notebook or staple them into a spelling book. For an already-made, ready to download and print spelling dictionary, I recommend The Measured Mom's Printable Spelling Dictionary (http://bit.ly/1qqo1O2).

Chapter 6: Hands-on Spelling Ideas

Traditional spelling looks something like this: see the words + write the words = memorize the words. Write the words five times each. Write the words in sentences. Work on spelling worksheets. The idea is that if we see the word a lot and write (or copy) the word a lot, then that particular string of letters will stick in our brain. Then we add on top of that the weekly spelling test. The goal is to ace the test. But what happens next week when our child needs to use one of those words in a writing assignment? You guessed. Typically, we find the word has not been moved to memory and is misspelled. With traditional spelling, spelling can become rather dull and boring for the student (and teacher). Spellers are mostly passive learners, simply empty containers to be filled with spelling knowledge. Kids often memorize the words for the test, but forget them after they have scored their 100's.

But let's contrast that with hands-on spelling, meaning that it appeals to the senses (multisensory) and engages the speller to interact with the words in a way that has great potential to help words "stick" in memory. In this chapter, you are sure to find some hands-on ideas for teaching spelling. We will explore how use manipulatives to spell, sort, and read as we get kids actively involved in learning both phonics and sight words.

Before exploring these ideas, remember that in order for any spelling instruction to be effective, we must be sure it is developmentally appropriate (Chapter 2). This means the child is "working at a level that is challenging, but not frustrating" (Telian, 1990). If we are teaching too many sight words for our child's level of development or asking kids to examine word patterns that they do not have the capacity to understand, yet, then hands-on spelling ideas may still lead to frustration for both the speller and you. Using developmentally appropriate practices alongside hands-on instruction is a *highly* powerful and effective tool for helping our spellers grow in their knowledge of spelling!

Please note that these hands-on spelling ideas are not meant to compete with one another. These ideas serve to complement each other. You may also decide to use idea one instead of another to fit the needs of your own child(ren).

Using Manipulatives

Hands-on spelling instruction most certainly includes asking our child to touch and manipulate letters and word chunks (such as *oa*). This is one of the beauties of *All About Spelling* (http://bit.ly/1cKezBJ). Included within the curriculum are phonogram letter tiles for the different sounds made in the English language. With young spellers, the letter tiles are perfect for practicing specific spelling strategies without the use of pencil and paper. While "the tiles don't take the place of spelling with paper and pencil, the tiles act as a fantastic learning tool that will enable your student to learn to spell more quickly and accurately and get to the real goal—writing" (http://bit.ly/1fkyzVS). The letter tiles are also good for struggling spellers who may be frustrated with needing to constantly erase spelling mistakes. With the letter tiles, mistakes can be "erased" with ease by moving that particular letter tile out of the way and moving another one in its place. The letter tiles are also color-coded to help demonstrate the different roles of letters (such as vowels versus consonants) for younger children and word meaning chunks (such as non- or –ful) for older spellers.

One of the effective things about the letter tiles from *All About Spelling* (as compared to using magnetic letters from your local dollar store) is that the word patterns or chunks are included together on one card. This means that instead of manipulating magnetic letters like this b-o-a-t, the child uses the tiles to manipulate *boat* like this: b-oa-t. Helping spellers see how vowel teams or word chunks work together as one unit makes remembering those patterns easier and in turn helps spellers read and spell those chunks more effectively.

Making Words, created by Pat Cunningham, is another strategy teachers can use to focus on spelling patterns within words. There are four parts to Making Words: (1) making words (2) sorting words, (3) transferring to reading, and (4) transferring to writing. Not all four parts need to happen at one sitting. On day one, you and your child could do parts one and two, saving parts three and four for another day.

Before you work with your child, gather letters (magnetic letters or letters on small pieces of paper will do) that work together to form a secret word. For our example, let's choose *umbrellas*. A little preparation is needed before the lesson begins as you need to brainstorm smaller words that can be made from *umbrellas*. To help in this process Pat Cunningham, in her book *Phonics They Use* (http://amzn.to/1fkyD81), suggests going to

http://www.wordplays.com and clicking on "Words in a Word."
While this tool can be helpful, I find that it does leave out a lot of
the smaller words you may want to use with the word. In our
example of *umbrellas*, I could use words such as (although I
could have chosen other patterns as well):

- *rub, sub, sum*

- *am, ram, bam, lamb*

- *all, ball, balls, mall, malls, small*

- *sell, bell, bells, smell*

Write each individual word from your list onto an index card.
These will be used during part one and part two of the lesson.

To begin part one of Making Words, hand the child all the letters
in a scrambled fashion without telling him the secret word. Begin
very simply by asking your child to create specific words using
letters from *umbrellas*. Start with "short, easy words and move to
longer, more complex words," ending by asking the child to try
and figure out what the secret word is (Cunningham, 2005). For
example, start by asking my child to make *rub*. As you move to
making and changing each word, give hints as to the spelling of
the word, such as "Use three letters to spell the word *rub*. Now,
change one letter of *rub* to make the word *sub*." Note that words

only change a little bit from one word to another. At the end of each row of words in the examples above, say something like, "Put all your letters back together and let's spell more words." With each word, give your child a few seconds to figure it out (giving helpful hints if needed) then display the word card with that word on it so the child can see it. If his answer is wrong, you will want him to fix it before you move to the next word. After all the words have been spelled, challenge him to use all the letter cards to figure out what the secret word is, providing hints if needed.

During part two of Making Words, take all the word cards (from your list of smaller words) and work on sorting them by pattern. In our particular lesson, I may guide the child to sort words by the word family chunks of –ub, -am, -all, and –ell. Depending upon your secret word and the developmental level of your child, you may sort words by beginning sounds, the vowel pattern in the middle, or root words. There are no hard and fast rules with this sort. Simply lay all the word cards out and ask your child, "What do you notice about these words? Let's group together the ones that are the same." If you already know that you want to feature word family patterns, let your child sort the words his way first. Acknowledge and praise his ideas, then guide him by asking, "Are there any words that share the same ending pattern as *all*? Let's see if we can find them all."

Parts three and four of Making Words are vitally important. These steps encourage kids to connect what they know about phonics to their reading and writing (spelling). We all know "it is much easier to teach children phonics than it is to actually get them to use it" in real reading and real writing (Cunningham, 2005). A simple way to do this is to pull out one of your word cards from part one and two of Making Words. Let's use *ball* as our example. Show the word card to your child, asking him to read it. Then do some role-playing together. "We know this word says *ball*. But what if you came to a word like this (spell *hall* on a piece of paper or dry erase board) in your reading? How can you use *ball* to help you figure out this word? (point to *hall*)" It may help to circle or highlight the –*all* chunk in both words so your child can explicitly see the shared pattern. You can do the same thing with transferring to writing. Show the word card containing *bell* and ask your child to read it. "Now, let's say you were writing a story about the beach and you needed to spell *shell*. How could you use *bell* to help you spell *shell*?" Work together to help him spell *shell* by providing helpful hints if needed.

You can find Making Words resources for grades K through five in chapter 8.

Use a MultiSensory Approach

Multisensory teaching is teaching that is done in such a manner that it appeals to the five senses. Instead of just telling someone about an avocado, we let them touch it, smell it, taste it, etc. The concept was borne out of Dr. Samuel Orton and Dr. Anna Gillingham's work with special needs students in the 1930's. This teaching method is now known as the Orton-Gillingham method or multisensory teaching. "The benefits of involving more than one sense during instruction is not limited to those with pronounced learning disabilities. Multi-sensory teaching is effective for all learners" (*The Struggling Reader* - Phonics Instruction Activities). When we incorporate and integrate the senses into learning, kids have lots of ways to "file" the new information in a way that makes sense to them. While multisensory teaching benefits all learners, children with special needs and those that struggle benefit greatly from this multisensory way of teaching.

Lively Letters is a reading program, specifically designed for those students who have a particular weakness in remembering their letter sounds or phonograms (groups of letters that make a sound). Their program contains phonics activities that appeal to auditory, kinesthetic, and visual learners all *at one time*. *Lively Letters* helps kids learn to spell by "using imagery, music,

75

humorous stories, body movements, and memory cues that create strong, lasting impressions" (Telian, 1990). Included in their program are letter and phonogram cards that have meaningful picture clues about the sound of the letter and how the letter sound should be made in the mouth.

Use Word Sorts

Word sorting is a practice in which spellers group word features by their category (by letter sounds, spelling patterns or word meanings). Sorting words helps kids "find order and similarities" among words. "When [kids] sort words, they are engaged in the active process of searching, comparing, contrasting, and analyzing" (Bear, et. al 2012). The goal of word sorting, also known as word study, is to help our kids create generalizations about how words and word patterns work by focusing on consistencies within the English language. Spellers can then take these generalizations and "apply to words they want to read or spell" (Williams, Cheri et al. 2009). For example, you may want to help your child compare and contrast words with a silent *e* feature on the end. He may already be familiar with the role of silent *e* in creating a long vowel sound in the word, but sees words like *have*, *prince*, and *raise* as words that "break the rules" of silent *e*. Instead of telling the student the roles that silent *e* has outright, especially at first, collect various words that feature these different roles. Write down the words you have collected separately on small cards. (You can also type them into a table on the computer and cut the words apart.)

Mix up all the word cards and place them in a pile at first. Ask your child to read through the words with you, making sure he can read all the words. Spread the words out on a workspace so he can see all the words at one time. Ask him to look at all the words and tell you what he notices about them. Besides the fact that they all have a silent *e*, are there any other similarities between some of the words? If your child is hesitant to answer, pick two words that share a similar silent *e* role (such as *have* and *love*) and ask him what he notices. Once he is able to verbalize a generalization (both words have a *–ve*), look for other words in the sort that share the same pattern. When all the words have been categorized by their spelling feature, create generalizations or observations about the roles that silent *e* plays in words. For more information on using word sorts for teaching spelling, visit my ten day series on Teaching Spelling through Word Study (http://bit.ly/1islIEr).

50 Hands-On Ways to Learn
Letter Names and Letter Sounds

Musical Alphabet   http://bit.ly/N1H1lL

Visualize Letters   http://bit.ly/1dJe8pc

Use Magnetic Letters   http://bit.ly/1cKfUIG

Use Sound Tubs   http://bit.ly/1nC58oJ

Match The Letters   http://bit.ly/1i5Itj9

Take It Outside   http://bit.ly/1gfdTmK

Play With Puzzles   http://bit.ly/1g2aK53

Play Read My Mind   http://bit.ly/1qqoQGv

Use Sensory Play   http://bit.ly/1oG9v0J

Slam Your Letters   http://bit.ly/1dJeEU2

Sort Letter Sounds   http://bit.ly/NT0eY8

Listen For Sounds In Words   http://bit.ly/1lPpdK6

Fish For Letters   http://bit.ly/1i1pSEb

Incorporate Toys And Manipulatives

                                    http://bit.ly/1cKgMwY

Build Your Letters With Yarn   http://bit.ly/1elD3Mo

Go On A Letter Hunt   http://bit.ly/1h7KpF9

Use Sticky Notes   http://bit.ly/1iuuBBU

Hop And Pop Letters   http://bit.ly/1ewgpAY

Use A Tunnel   http://bit.ly/1iFycJ4

Make A Sticky Wall   http://bit.ly/1kP4S7e

Alphabet Sound Jump   http://bit.ly/1iFyVhF

Match Letters To Sounds   http://bit.ly/1kP4VA2

Write In Salt   http://bit.ly/PxqY1f

Use A Pocket Chart   http://bit.ly/1kmTvkc

Hide Your Letters   http://bit.ly/1i8demW

Letter Toss   http://bit.ly/1ihNlSn

Form Letters With Playdough   http://bit.ly/1kP55aH

Use A Felt Board   http://bit.ly/1hfSR5x

ABC Scavenger Hunt For Sounds   http://bit.ly/1m0vKBG

Make Rope Letters   http://bit.ly/1ihNCEU

Eat With Letters   http://bit.ly/1fA0h5S

Play With Foam Letters   http://bit.ly/1fVQWWZ

Use Alphabet Cookie Cutters   http://bit.ly/PxrjRP

Use Letter Sticks   http://bit.ly/1hfT4Wj

Make ABC Frisbees With Lids   http://bit.ly/1iFzF6u

Make Yarn Books   http://bit.ly/1kP5lqc

DIY Alphabet Milk Bottle Tops   http://bit.ly/O7pB8E

Get Active!   http://bit.ly/1i8dClp

Use Alphabet Stickers   http://bit.ly/PxrBIc

Use Magazines And/Or Newspapers http://bit.ly/1fVRmwz

Make Alphabet Soup   http://bit.ly/1oQpeKN

Play Runaway Alphabet   http://bit.ly/1oQpg5q

Make Letter Collages   http://bit.ly/O7qwpC

Use Push Pins   http://bit.ly/1gnEL43

Pound The Letters   http://bit.ly/1gnEOww

Alphabet Bingo   http://bit.ly/1iFART6

Play ABC Tic-Tac-Toe   http://bit.ly/1i8e2s1

Make An ABC Scrapbook   http://bit.ly/OoAXVG

Make ABC Stairs   http://bit.ly/1hfU2Sc

Use Flashcards In Fun Ways   http://bit.ly/1hfU4cV

50 Hands-On Ways to Teaching Spelling
(Phonics and Sight Words)

Most of these online activities can be adapted for sight words AND for phonics skills.

Use Sidewalk Chalk   http://bit.ly/1gtKzVU

Spell Words With Lego Bricks   http://bit.ly/1i8eO8D

Ride Your Bike Over Words   http://bit.ly/1lChQCB

Eat Your Words   http://bit.ly/O7t9rr

Slam Your Words   http://bit.ly/1nngBvT

Play Soccer With Words   http://bit.ly/1gtLEgg

Jump To Letters As You Spell Words

                                  http://bit.ly/1dVx3gv

Spell Words With Beads   http://bit.ly/OoBFlG

Stamp The Words   http://bit.ly/1kmXpJS

Spell With Cars   http://bit.ly/1i8fef1

Swim With Words   http://bit.ly/1gtLEgg

Spell With Cups   http://bit.ly/1gtLF3O

Play I Spy	http://bit.ly/1qzQnFp
Paint Words	http://bit.ly/1lCicJw
Flip A Word	http://bit.ly/1cXjXvD
Spell Words In The Bathtub	http://bit.ly/1m0zgMf
Play Spelling BINGO	http://bit.ly/1ewlBVC
Cut And Glue Word Patterns	http://bit.ly/1fu3wXK
Go Sponge Bowling With Words	http://bit.ly/1ihRTrU
Spell With Magnetic Letters	http://bit.ly/1cXk9uU
Spin For Words	http://bit.ly/1nUw3fH
Play Tic-Tac-Toe	http://bit.ly/1kmY3Hm
Knock Down Words	http://bit.ly/1hfWvfw
Play Dice Games	http://bit.ly/1iFDvrP
Use Sticky Notes	http://bit.ly/1iFDAvO
Card Games	http://bit.ly/1qzQP6G
Slide Your Words	http://bit.ly/1oQwdDz
Bump Your Words	http://bit.ly/1ewuzlw

Use Paper Plates   http://bit.ly/1oQyM8K

Spell With Bottle Caps   http://bit.ly/1oQyIFT

Write Words In Shaving Cream   http://bit.ly/1ewuu1b

Reuse Toilet Paper Rolls   http://bit.ly/1cXqgzf

Incorporate Sensory Play   http://bit.ly/1ewupuF

Use A Muffin Tin   http://bit.ly/1g6vmh7

Spell Words In Dry Oatmeal, Cornmeal, Rice, Or Salt
                                    http://bit.ly/1oQyBdk

Sort Words   http://bit.ly/1m0G6Bv

Create And Use a Moveable Alphabet
                                    http://bit.ly/1i1aiJ1

Use Stickers   http://bit.ly/1kbPO0N

Go On A Treasure Hunt   http://bit.ly/1gnMeAb

Crayon Rubbing   http://bit.ly/1fu8y6C

Make Magnetic Words   http://bit.ly/1gnMbEc

Build Words With Puzzles   http://bit.ly/O7DKCR

Sift And Spell   http://bit.ly/1m0zSSc

Stomp Your Words   http://bit.ly/O7vEdk

Use A Board Game   http://bit.ly/1i1akk1

Use A Pocket Chart   http://bit.ly/1qqskJa

Color Your Words   http://bit.ly/1m0zYJr

Use Plastic Easter Eggs   http://bit.ly/1lqGd69

Word Hunt Through Books   http://bit.ly/1fVXgOc

Sort Real And Silly Words   http://bit.ly/1iFLQjA

Chapter 7: The Relationship between Spelling and Reading

Spelling is just as important to reading as reading is to spelling. They both share mutual benefits for our kids.

Reading Helps Kids Remember Spellings

Reading can help kids remember the correct spellings of words. Multiple exposure to words through real reading helps to solidify the spellings of words. When kids see a word through multiple and meaningful contexts, it begins to stick. The same is true of reading and word games (bit.ly/1ndN8Va). While reading, we can also help our spellers be on the lookout for words that have a particular pattern in them. We can look out for "unfamiliar words and make a mental note of the spelling" (http://bit.ly/1ndN8Va). It is important to note that just like spelling instruction needs to be on a developmentally appropriate level, so does reading. If we are immersing our kids in books that are too difficult for them to read, reading can lose its powerful effect on spelling. While we want to read a variety of books aloud to our kids, we want reading instruction to be on their "just right" reading level (http://thisreadingmama.com/2014/01/12/how-to-choose-just-right-books/).

Reading Can Help Kids Recognize Misspelled Words

As our spellers are given multiple and meaningful exposure to words through reading, they begin to remember the conventional spellings of high frequency words. They also begin to recognize when the word is spelled incorrectly, even in their own writing. They may ask themselves if the misspelled word looks right. This is such a great by-product of reading! "Even when [spellers] misspell words, they restrict their letter choices to those they have seen in [real] words rather than phonemically equivalent alternatives" (Ehri, 1997). For example, when a child needs to spell *cage*, his misspelling would not include CAJ because he has not seen any words in the English language ending with *j*.

When an older speller (beyond the Emergent spelling stage) does not catch a misspelled word in his writing, sometimes it helps to ask him to re-read his own writing. As he comes to his misspelled word, he will usually catch it and fix it because it does not look right. The Try It! page in the appendix is a great tool to help kids spell the word a couple of ways to see which way looks right. If he is unable to figure it out the correct spelling, he can bring it to an adult for help.

Spelling Instruction Helps Build Fluency and Comprehension

A large portion of learning to read with fluency is the ability to recognize words quickly and easily so the mind can be freed up to focus on understanding the text (comprehension). "The reason why spelling helps reading is that spelling instruction helps to cultivate students' knowledge of the alphabetic system which benefits processes used in reading" (Ehri, 1997). Taking time to focus on spelling instruction requires the child to zero in on words by their sequence and their patterns; not by using partial cues (like many young readers do), but by soaking in all the pattern and meaning cues the word has to offer. When spelling instruction is developmentally appropriate and strategic, it crosses over to reading because it is easier for our spellers to recognize words quickly and without much effort. This leads to better fluency.

Reading and Spelling Both Build Vocabulary

As kids move from the younger grades to the older elementary grades, reading becomes less about learning to read and more about reading to learn. Word meanings within texts, especially non-fiction texts, can become a bit harder to decipher, having a negative effect on comprehension. As kids grow in their spelling abilities, we move more into learning to spell by meaning. Prefixes and suffixes as well as Greek roots and Latin stems are studied. Spelling instruction at this level helps our kids understand that spelling patterns and meaning are directly connected. Studying these word meanings gives our readers concrete word meaning strategies that they can apply to reading and understanding more difficult vocabulary words.

Spelling + Reading = Writing

Spellers use reading to help them write. How so? As spellers write their own compositions, we encourage them to re-read their writing. One of the purposes of re-reading is to check for meaning and to revise the text. We also encourage writers to re-read their own writing to check for spelling. "To the extent that readers do this…reading as well as spelling contribute to the final spelling product" (Ehri, 1997).

Spelling Matters to the Reader

While "it is important for children to look at [and learn how to spell] words in isolation so that they can examine the patterns in words without the distractions of context," we do not want to stay out of context too long (Stahl, Duffy, & Stahl, 1998). Spelling has an authentic purpose. A purpose even beyond reading. While it does have direct benefits with reading, spelling empowers a writer's voice and message. Spelling does matter to the reader. Misspellings can distract readers from the writer's message. Correct spelling is a courtesy to the reader. We must never lose sight of that truth when teaching kids to spell.

Chapter 8: Exceptional Products and Resources
for Teaching Spelling

Words Their Way

Words Their Way is a product I have personally used for about ten years as I taught in the classroom, as a reading tutor, and now as a homeschooling mom. The sorts are quick and easy to implement, hands-on, and developmentally appropriate for teaching spelling. The following products are ones I would recommend to anyone teaching kids to spell, from the Pre-K ages through high school. You can read my review of *Words Their Way*'s products on my blog (http://bit.ly/1fKVj6o).

Words Their Way for PreK-K   http://amzn.to/1h7KFEh

Words Their Way: Word Study for Phonics, Vocabulary, and Spelling Instruction   http://amzn.to/OeDhyo

Letter and Picture Sorts for Emergent Spellers

http://amzn.to/1qqpP9I

Word Sorts for Letter Name-Alphabetic Spellers

http://amzn.to/1cKhxG7

Word Sorts for Within Word Pattern Spellers

http://amzn.to/1iurtWH

Word Sorts for Syllables and Affixes Spellers

http://amzn.to/1g2bXtd

Word Sorts for Derivational Relations Spellers

http://amzn.to/OeGk9J

All About Spelling

All About Spelling (http://bit.ly/1cKezBJ) is a part of a larger company called *All About Learning Press*. It was created and designed out of a desire to help struggling readers and spellers learn in a way that best suits their learning needs. While *All About Spelling* works great for struggling spellers, it can be used for any child. *All About Spelling* starts with letters and letter sounds and moves into studying Greek and Latin roots. If you want to learn more about *All About Spelling* and their other program *All About Reading*, feel free to read the online articles listed in the Other Helpful Online Articles below. You can also read my review of *All About Reading* (http://bit.ly/1dJg3tL).

Lively Letters

Lively Letters is a wonderful phonics program, especially for older students who are really struggling to learn phonics. The program mixes music, humor, poetry, and meaningful pictures to help kids learn not only their letter sounds, but how those sounds are produced in the mouth. Kids can then apply those sounds to early reading and beyond. To read more about *Lively Letters*, read my review (http://bit.ly/1isqGB3) or visit their website (http://bit.ly/1g2f98e).

Sight Words You Can See

Sight Words You Can See is a sister company to *Lively Letters*. *Sight Words You Can See* helps those students struggling to learn sight words do it in a fun and visual way with memorable mnemonic strategies. To learn more, read my review (http://bit.ly/PkW8sO) of *Sight Words You Can See* or visit their website (http://www.readingwithtlc.com/site-words.html).

Making Words for Kindergarten by Patricia Cunningham and
Dorothy P. Hall   http://amzn.to/1lPqm4e

Making Words for 1st Grade by Patricia Cunningham and
Dorothy P. Hall   http://amzn.to/1lqCKoh

Making Words for 2nd Grade by Patricia Cunningham and
Dorothy P. Hall   http://amzn.to/1iurQQY

Making Words for 3rd Grade by Patricia Cunningham and
Dorothy P. Hall   http://amzn.to/1ndRiw2

Making Words for 4th Grade by Patricia Cunningham and
Dorothy P. Hall   http://amzn.to/1kbNeYz

Making Words for 5th Grade by Patricia Cunningham and
Dorothy P. Hall   http://amzn.to/1dJgkNx

Other Helpful Online Articles and Posts

Why We Teach Reading and Spelling Separately
http://blog.allaboutlearningpress.com/why-we-teach-reading-
and-spelling-separately/

How to Handle Misspelled Words
http://www.allaboutlearningpress.com/how-to-handle-
misspelled-words

How to Correct Spelling Mistakes

http://www.allaboutlearningpress.com/how-to-correct-spelling-mistakes

How to Teach Spelling with Letter Tiles

http://www.allaboutlearningpress.com/how-to-teach-spelling-with-letter-tiles

Effective Spelling Strategies

http://www.allaboutlearningpress.com/effective-spelling-strategies

Invented Spelling and Spelling Development

http://www.readingrockets.org/article/267

No More Friday Spelling Tests!

http://www.readingrockets.org/blog/27769

10 days of Teaching Spelling through Word Study

http://thisreadingmama.com/2012/10/13/teaching-spelling-word-study/

A Better Way to Teach Spelling

http://www.themeasuredmom.com/a-better-way-to-teach-spelling/

Flip a Word with Word Families
http://thisreadingmama.com/2013/11/01/help-readers-blend-words/

1-2-3 Spell It! http://thisreadingmama.com/2013/10/06/short-vowel-spelling-game/

FAQ and Literacy Resources
http://thisreadingmama.com/2013/07/18/faq-literacy-resources-for-parents/

Literacy Terms Defined for Parents
http://thisreadingmama.com/2013/11/14/literacy-terms-defined-for-parents/

10 Things Struggling Readers Need
http://thisreadingmama.com/2011/06/20/new-series-on-struggling-readers/

Reading the Alphabet- a free reading curriculum for emergent readers with beginning practice for reading and spelling.
http://thisreadingmama.com/free-reading-curriculum/reading-the-alphabet-prek-curriculum/

Free BOB Book printables for Set 1 through 5
http://thisreadingmama.com/2013/01/07/free-bob-book-printables/

No-Mess Products for Beginning Spellers

MagnaDoodle   http://amzn.to/1kHXIBN

AquaDoodle   http://amzn.to/PkSoHG

Glow Station   http://amzn.to/1cKibDw

Color Wonder   http://amzn.to/NT29M4

Foam Bath Letters   http://amzn.to/1fQCDD4

Jumbo Magnetic Letters   http://amzn.to/1oGaYEj

Magnetic Letter Tracers

Uppercase   http://amzn.to/OeGUV7

Lowercase   http://amzn.to/1ndRCej

Hands-On Products for Spelling Instruction

Alphabet Puzzles   http://amzn.to/PGJNiJ

ABC Cookie Letters   http://amzn.to/1kHXVVD

Letter Construction Kit   http://amzn.to/1elEyKr

Letter Stickers   http://amzn.to/1i5KKea

Leapfrog Word Factory Fridge Set   http://amzn.to/1nC8mbQ

Thinkfun's What's Gnu   http://amzn.to/1fkCu4W

Thinkfun's Zingo Sight Words   http://amzn.to/1g2cX0q

Bananagrams   http://amzn.to/1lqE0b1

Scrabble, Jr.   http://amzn.to/1qqqWWZ

Sidewalk Chalk   http://amzn.to/1kHY637

Wikki Sticks   http://amzn.to/1isoJVn

Letter Stamps   http://amzn.to/1fQCUGe

Letter Beads   http://amzn.to/1elFD4U

Photo Stacking Blocks – insert letters, word patterns, or other
word features   http://amzn.to/1i19RhD

Pocket Chart   http://amzn.to/1lPs0Tu

Finger pointers   http://amzn.to/1dJhIiU

Magnetic letters   http://amzn.to/1gfgrkH

Cookie Sheets   http://amzn.to/1h7MhxT

Playdough Letters   http://amzn.to/1dJhBnM

Highlighters   http://amzn.to/1h7Mcdx

Scented Markers   http://amzn.to/1fQD8Nr

Post-It Notes   http://amzn.to/1cPAq58

Dry Erase Boards:

Large   http://amzn.to/1fQD7t4

Small   http://amzn.to/1fQD7ZR

Dry erase markers   http://amzn.to/1fQD4NQ

Sentence Strips   http://amzn.to/1fkBzS8

Plastic Sleeve Protectors (slip pages in and use a dry erase marker)   http://amzn.to/1kHYgaP

Conclusion

Teaching kids to spell does not have to be a daunting task. When kids are taught at their developmental stage in meaningful and hands-on ways, spelling is given life and purpose. The end goal of spelling instruction is not a perfect grade on that Friday spelling test. Instead, it is to equip kids to become better readers and writers, for now and for a lifetime. That, my friends, is the power of teaching kids to spell.

Appendix

Extra Charts and Printable Resources

Beginning Letter Sound Chart

Consonant Blends and Digraphs Chart

Common Single Syllable Vowel Patterns

Word Feature Charts for Each Developmental Stage

Spelling Checklist for Evaluating Spellings Within Written Products

My Word Family Dictionary

My Word Pattern Dictionary

My Spelling Dictionary

Try It! Page

Download and print the following charts using this link:

http://thisreadingmama.com/wp-content/uploads/2014/03/Teaching-Kids-to-Spell-Printable-Resource-Pack.pdf

Beginning Letter Sound Chart

🍎	apple	**9**	nine
🎈	balloon	🐙	octopus
🚗	car	🍕	pizza
🐕	dog	🔲	quilt
🥚	egg	〰️	rope
🐟	fish	☀️	sun
🦍	gorilla	**10**	ten
🚁	helicopter	☂️	umbrella
❄️	igloo	🧹	vacuum
🧃	juice	🍉	watermelon
🪁	kite	📦	box*
🦁	lion	🧶	yarn
🧤	mitten	🦓	zebra

Download and print these charts using this link: http://bit.ly/1dMcUM1

Consonant Blends and Digraphs

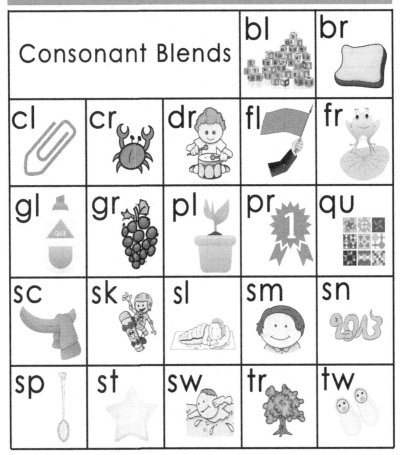

Consonant Blends — bl, br, cl, cr, dr, fl, fr, gl, gr, pl, pr, qu, sc, sk, sl, sm, sn, sp, st, sw, tr, tw

Consonant Digraphs

ch, ph, sh, th, wh

Download and print these charts using this link: http://bit.ly/1dMcUM1

Common Single Syllable Vowel Patterns

short vowels
cat
red
fish
box
sun

bossy r
car
perch
girl
horse
burn

crawl
ball
pause

long a patterns
cake
paint
play

long i patterns
kite
light
tie
fly

other vowels
book
coin
boy
cloud
cow

long e patterns
tree
leaf
baby*

long o patterns
rope
boat
snow
toe

long u patterns
cube
stew
glue
moon
juice

Download and print these charts using this link: http://bit.ly/1dMcUM1

Word Feature Charts for Each Developmental Stage

The following charts contain phonics features or word meanings for teaching spelling in the developmental stages (from Chapter 2). The name of the stage beside each chart (in parentheses) is the stage at which a speller would typically be ready to learn about the *spelling* of the phonics features or word meanings. Please note that spellers will be able to read and/or comprehend these word patterns and meanings before they can spell them independently.

This is by no means an exhaustive list. If you are looking for more ideas, you can find them in Appendix E of *Words Their Way*.

Download and print these charts using this link: http://bit.ly/1dMcUM1

Blends and Digraphs

(Late Letter Name-Alphabetic Spellers)

Common Blends

*A blend is two letters, put together, and you hear BOTH sounds.

R Blends: br, dr, fr, gr, pr, tr

L Blends: bl, fl, gl, pl, sl

S Blends: sc, sk, sl, sm, sn, sp

Other Blends: tw, qu

Common Digraphs

*A digraph is two letters, put together, and you hear ONE sound.

sh, th, ch, ph, wr, kn, gn

Download and print these charts using this link: http://bit.ly/1dMcUM1

Common Word Families

(Late Letter Name-Alphabetic to Within Word Pattern)

Common Short Vowel Word Family Patterns
Short a: -at, -an, -am, -ap, -and, -ash, -ank
Short e: -et, -en, -ed, -ell, -est, -ent
Short i: -ig, -it, -in, -id, -ill, -ick, -ing, -ink
Short o: -ot, -og, -op, -ock, -ong
Short u: -ut, -ug, -un, -um, -ub, -uck, -ump, -uff, -ust

Common Long Vowel Word Family Patterns
Long a: -ake, -ane, -ate, -ale, -ade, -age, -ange, -ain, -ail, -ait, -ay
Long e: -ee, -eek, -een, -eed, -eel, -eep, -ean, -ead, -eak, -eal
Long i: -ike, -ime, -ite, -ipe, -ise, -ice, -ide, -ie, -ight, -ind, -y
Long o: -ose, -ome, -ope, -ote, -oke, -one, -oat, -oak, -oal, -oast
Long u: -ude, -ute, -ue, -ew

Common Word Family Patterns (Other Vowels)
-all, -ar, -aw, -ause
-ir
-out, -ow, -own, -oo, -oom, -ood

Short, Long, and Other Vowel Patterns
(Late Letter Name-Alphabetic through Within Word Pattern)

Short Vowel Patterns
Short a: single a (cat)
Short e: single e (bed), ea (head)
Short i: single i (pig)
Short o: single o (hot)
Short u: single u (cut)
Long Vowel Patterns*
Long a: a_e (name), ai (train), ay (play), ei (eight), ey (they)
Long e: ee (green), ea (bead), e_e (these), final e (she), ie (chief)
Long i: i_e (kite), igh (high), ie (pie), single i (find), final y (why), ye (bye)
Long o: o_e (note), oa (goat), oe (toe), ow (snow), single o (told)
Long u: u_e (mule), ue (blue), ew (grew), ui (fruit), oo (moon), final o (to)
*Within Word Pattern Spellers
Other Vowel Patterns*
R-Influenced Vowels: ar (park), er (perch), ir (first), or (fork), ur (burn)
W-Influenced Vowels: w+a (walk), w+o (work)
Other Vowels: aw (saw), au (pause), al (salt), oo (good), ou (sound), ow (clown), oi (coin), oy (boy)
*Within Word Pattern Spellers

Download and print these charts using this link: http://bit.ly/1dMcUM1

Inflected Endings and Syllable Juncture Patterns

(Syllable Juncture Spellers)

Inflected Endings
-ed (jumped), -ing (jumping), -s (jumps), -es (mixes)
Patterns that Govern Adding Inflected Endings (Syllable Juncture)
No change when adding to word (jump + ing = jumping or play + s = plays) Double when adding to the word (shop + ing = shopping) Drop the silent e when adding to the word (drive + ing = driving) Change the y to i and add –es (baby + s = babies)
Unaccented Syllables
-ar (dollar), -er (bigger), -or (doctor), -le (table), -el (camel), -en (broken), -on (wagon), -in (napkin), -ain (mountain)

Common Affixes

(Syllable Juncture through Derivational Relations Spellers)

Common Prefixes in Alphabetical Order
bi- (bifocals), de- (deflate), en- (entrance), ex- (excavator), fore- (forehead), dis- (dislike), in- (meaning not/incorrect), in- (meaning in/inbounds), mis- (misplace), non- (nonsense), oct- (octagon), post- (postpone), pre- (preschool), re- (reuse), semi- (semicircle), sub- (subheading), tri- (tricycle), un- (unclear)
Common Suffixes in Alphabetical Order
-er (bigger), -est (biggest), -ful (thankful), -less (fearless), -ly (loudly), -ness (kindness), -y (windy)
Harder Suffixes*
-tion (nation), -sion (vision), -sure (pleasure), –ture (adventure), -ent (vs. –ant (, -ence (independence) vs. –ance (attendance), -ible (horrible) vs. –able (comfortable) *Derivational Relations

Download and print these charts using this link: http://bit.ly/1dMcUM1

Roots and Base Words- Latin Stems and Greek Roots

(Derivational Relations Spellers)

Harder Prefixes

---

anti- (antibiotic), auto- (autobiography), cent- (century), circum- (circumstance), inter- (interstate), intra- (intramural), mal- (malice), mono- (monogram), multi- (multitask), peri- (periodical), poly- (polytheistic), pro- (pronounce), super- (superficial), trans- (transport)

Examples of Latin Stems and Greek Roots

---

bene (beneficial), corp (corpse), duct (aqueduct), form (format), junct (junction), mal (malice), ped (pedestrian), port (transportation), sect (insect), terra (terrain), vid (video)

arch (architect), bio (biology), cosm (cosmic), derm (dermatologist), graph (telegraph), homo (homophone), pan (pandemic), photo (photograph), tele (telephone)

Download and print these charts using this link: http://bit.ly/1dMcUM1

Spelling Checklist for Evaluating Spellings within Written Products

	Word Features Look for these word features in your child's writing.	Demonstrates Clear Understanding (√)	Not a Complete Understanding (√)	Notes
Emergent Speller	beginning consonants			
Emergent Speller	ending consonants			
Letter Name Alphabetic Speller	short vowels			
Letter Name Alphabetic Speller	blends			
Letter Name Alphabetic Speller	digraphs			
Within Word Pattern Speller	long vowel patterns			
Within Word Pattern Speller	other vowel patterns			
Within Word Pattern Speller	inflected endings			

Download and print these charts using this link: http://bit.ly/1dMcUM1

	Word Features Look for these word features in your child's writing.	Demonstrates Clear Understanding (√)	Not a Complete Understanding (√)	Notes
Syllable Juncture Speller	syllable juncture			
	unaccented final syllables			
Derivational Relations Speller	common prefixes and suffixes			
	harder prefixes and suffixes			
	Latin stems and Greek roots			

Download and print these charts using this link: http://bit.ly/1dMcUM1

My
Word Family
Dictionary

Name: _____

Download and print these charts using this link: http://bit.ly/1dMcUM1

As you read and study more words in this word family, write them on the lines below. Add this page to your Word Family Dictionary to help you read and spell the words in this family.

family

114

Download and print these charts using this link: http://bit.ly/1dMcUM1

My
Word Pattern
Dictionary

Name: _____

Download and print these charts using this link: http://bit.ly/1dMcUM1

As you read and study more words with this word pattern (word chunk), write them on the lines below. Add this page to your Word Pattern Dictionary to help you read and spell the words with this word chunk.

pattern

Download and print these charts using this link: http://bit.ly/1dMcUM1

My
Spelling
Dictionary

Name: _____

Download and print these charts using this link: http://bit.ly/1dMcUM1

Write a letter of the alphabet in the box to the right. After you have studied a sight word that begins with this letter, write it on one of the lines below. As you study more words that start with this letter, write those, too. Add this to your Spelling Dictionary to create a dictionary of spelling words.

letter

Download and print these charts using this link: http://bit.ly/1dMcUM1

Try It! Page: When you get to a word you do not know how to spell, try spelling it twice yourself. If it still does not look right, then take the word to an adult to spell.

Try It Once	Try It Twice	Ask an Adult

119

Download and print these charts using this link: http://bit.ly/1dMcUM1

Resources Cited

Bear, et al. (2012). *Words Their Way: Word Study for Phonics, Vocabulary, and Spelling Instruction.* Portland, ME: Pearson Education, Inc.

Calkins, Lucy. (1994). *The Art of Teaching Writing.* Portsmouth, NH: Heinemann.

Cunningham, Patricia. (2005). *Phonics They Use.* Portland, ME: Pearson Education, Inc.

Eckenwiler & Eckenwiler. (2007). Fluency. The Struggling Reader, Inc. (http://www.thestrugglingreader.net/)

Ehri, Linnea C. (2005). Learning to Read Words: Theory, Findings, and Issues. *Scientific Studies of Reading*, 9, 167-188.

Ehri, Linnea C. (1997). *Learning to Spell: Research, Theory, and Practice Across Languages.* Mahwah, NJ: Lawrence Erlbaum Associates, Inc.

Ehri, Linnea & McCormick, Sandra. (1999). Phases of Word Learning: Implications for Instruction with Delayed and Disabled Readers. *Reading and Writing Quarterly*, 14, 135-163

Hauerwas, Laura B. & Walker, Joanne. (2004). What Can Childs' Spelling of *Running* and *Jumped* Tell Us About Their

Need for Spelling Instruction? *The Reading Teacher*, 58, 168-176.

Invernizzi, Marcie A., Abouzeid, Mary P., & Bloodgood, Janet W. (1997). Integrated Word Study: Spelling, Grammar, and Meaning in the Language Arts Classroom. *Language Arts*, 74, 185-192.

Johnston, Francine R. (1999). The Timing and Teaching of Word Families. *The Reading Teacher,* 53, 64-75.

Johnston, et. al. (2014). *Words Their Way for PreK-K*. Portland, ME: Pearson Education, Inc.

McKenna & Stahl. (2003). *Assessment for Reading Instruction*. New York: The Guilford Press.

Morris, Darrell. (2005). *The Howard Street Tutoring Manual*. New York: The Guilford Press.

Newlands, Michelle. (2011). Intentional Spelling: Seven Steps to Eliminate Guessing. *The Reading Teacher*, 64, 531-534.

Rasinski, Timothy, Rupley, William H., Nichols, William D. (). Two Essential Ingredients: Phonics and Fluency Getting to Know Each Other. *The Reading Teacher*, 62, 257-260.

Rippel, Marie. (2013). *All About Spelling: Level 1 Teacher's Manual.* WI: All About Learning Press, Inc.

Rippel, Marie. Various Blog Posts and Articles, Retrieved February, 2014 from

http://www.allaboutlearningpress.com/list-on-monday-test-on-friday-spelling

http://www.allaboutlearningpress.com/how-to-correct-spelling-mistakes

http://www.allaboutlearningpress.com/which-spelling-level-should-we-start-with

http://blog.allaboutlearningpress.com/using-all-about-spelling-with-older-students/

http://www.allaboutlearningpress.com/how-to-teach-spelling-with-letter-tiles

Schickedanze, Judith A., Chay, Soyoung, Gopin, P., Sheng, L.L., Song, Soo-Mi, & Wild, Nancy. (1990). Preschoolers and Academics: Some Thoughts. *Young Children*, 46, 4-13.

Stahl, Steven.A., Duffy-Hester, Ann.M., & Stahl, Katherine A.D. (1998). Everything You Wanted to Know About Phonics (But Were Afraid to Ask). *Reading Research Quarterly*, 33, 338-355.

Telian, Nancy. (1990) *Lively Letters Instruction Manuel.* USA: Telian-Cas Learning Concepts, Inc.

Telian, Nancy A. & Castagnozzi, Penny A. Various Articles, Retrieved February, 2014 from

http://www.readingwithtlc.com/lively-letters.html
http://www.readingwithtlc.com/site-words.html

Williams, Cheri & Lundstrom Ruth P. (2007). Strategy and Instruction During Word Study and Interactive Writing Activities. *The Reading Teacher*, 61, 204-212.

Williams, Cheri et al. (2009). Word Study Instruction in the K-2 Classroom. *The Reading Teacher*, 62, 570-578.

Yopp, Hallie K. & Yopp, Ruth H. (2000). Supporting Phonemic Awareness Development in the Classroom. *The Reading Teacher*, 54, 130-143.

About the Author

Becky Spence traded in her public school teaching career to follow God's call to be at home with her children. As a stay-at-home mom, she finished her M.Ed. in Elementary Reading and tutored struggling readers in her home. She integrated spelling instruction into her tutoring sessions and saw amazing results with struggling spellers and readers. In the fall of 2010, Becky began homeschooling. She knew this was God's call on her life, and after wrestling with it a bit, she felt at peace. But homeschooling was a little lonelier than expected. She desired to share her ideas and connect with other educators and parents. In February of 2011, she started her literacy blog, This Reading Mama, where she shares practical tips, hands-on activities, printables, and reading curricula. In January of 2013, she wrote her first book, *How to Choose "Just Right" Books: Helping Kids Grow as Readers.*

http://thisreadingmama.com/2014/01/12/how-to-choose-just-right-books/

You can connect with Becky at

Google + https://plus.google.com/+BeckySpence/posts,

Pinterest http://www.pinterest.com/thisreadingmama,

Facebook http://www.facebook.com/thisreadingmama,

Twitter http://www.twitter.com/thisreadingmom,

or subscribe by email to http://thisreadingmama.com/.

Made in the USA
Columbia, SC
08 September 2020